FRESH MEXICAN

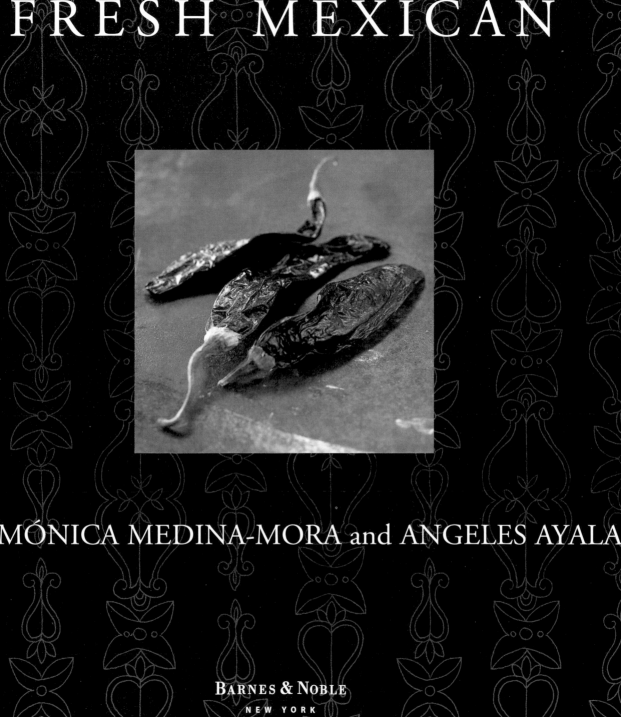

MÓNICA MEDINA-MORA and ANGELES AYALA

BARNES & NOBLE

NEW YORK

Note

Food and Drug Administration advises that eggs should not be consumed raw. This book contains some dishes made with raw or lightly cooked eggs. It is prudent for vulnerable people such as pregnant and nursing mothers, invalids, the elderly, babies, and young children to avoid uncooked or lightly cooked dishes made with eggs. Once prepared, these dishes should be kept refrigerated and used promptly.

This book includes dishes made with nuts and nut derivatives. It is advisable for those with known allergic reactions to nuts and nut derivatives and those who may be potentially vulnerable to these allergies, such as pregnant and nursing mothers, invalids, the elderly, babies, and children to avoid dishes made with nuts and nut oils. It is also prudent to check the labels of pre-prepared ingredients for the possible inclusion of nut derivatives.

Ovens should be preheated to the specified temperature—if using a fan-assisted oven, follow the manufacturer's instructions for adjusting the time and the temperature.

Fresh herbs should be used unless otherwise stated.
Medium eggs should be used unless otherwise stated.

Contents

Introduction

Be prepared for a really unforgettable assault on your senses, for authentic Mexican cooking offers one of the most exciting culinary experiences in the world. Explosions of color, captivating aromas, deliciously rich flavors, and stunning textures combine to produce a distinctive and truly great celebration of food. The range of dishes, ingredients, and regional specialties to be savored reflect the vibrant culture of Mexico and its origins in the pre-Hispanic world.

Essential ingredients

Mexican cuisine benefits from its reliance on fresh ingredients. The land of many different types of chili, Mexico has long been the provider of important ingredients for the Old World: corn, an essential staple and regarded as a sacred food by the Native Americans, vanilla beans, avocados, tomatoes, and the revered cacao bean—the essential ingredient for chocolate—which at one time served as currency among the native traders. The arrival of the Spanish Conquistadores in the 16th century enriched and enhanced the national menu by introducing their own preferred ingredients, such as pork, beef, lamb, chicken, chickpeas, cabbages, sugar cane, and citrus fruits. Over time, a fusion of the two cultures took place and culminated in a unique cuisine that boasts a stunning range of dishes, as you will discover from the selection in this book.

Mexican fare can claim its place as one of the forefathers of the global kitchen, having introduced the world to many of the ingredients used in its daily cooking. How would Mediterranean dishes manage without tomatoes? As for the prospect of dessert menus deprived of chocolate, it simply doesn't bear thinking about! And try to imagine how different some of your favorite dishes from Southeast Asian cuisines would taste without the distinctive heat and piquancy that chili brings to them.

Enriched by regionality

Regional variation in cooking techniques, ingredients, and flavorings is one of the key factors that makes Mexican cooking such an exciting cuisine. The country has defined regional boundaries, creating self-contained communities that use locally grown ingredients with local cooking techniques and finishing touches for many of the national dishes.

Healthy traditions

A lesser-known contribution that Mexican cuisine brings to the global kitchen is a wide choice of wholesome and nutritious meals, prepared with healthy cooking methods and the right combination of ingredients to guarantee balanced meal plans. Many dishes are still prepared in the same healthy ways that were once practiced before the arrival of the Spanish. Steaming, poaching, and boiling are some of the most common methods used, and nothing is thrown away, so cooking liquids and the valuable nutrients they contain are incorporated in the dishes. Another plus point is that sauces are very healthy, as they are commonly thickened either by reduction or with ground seeds or corn, without the addition of butter or cream. This is why Mexican cookery fits so well with the modern-day focus on the pursuit of physical wellbeing and healthy eating.

Cook, eat, and enjoy!

Mexican cuisine cannot fail to captivate your taste buds, entertain your guests, and broaden your culinary know-how. Enjoy the discovery of new ingredients and new methods, and savor the experience of Mexican cooking!

Eating the Mexican way

For the full, authentic experience of eating *a la mexicana*, a whistlestop guide through the country's daily eating habits helps to set the scene for Mexican cooking and puts the dishes that are described in the book in context.

The big breakfast

The working day in Mexico either starts very early in the morning with a light breakfast of coffee and a sweet roll, or slightly later with a full-blown *desayuno*.

This wholesome and nutritional breakfast begins with a plate of fresh seasonal fruit and a glass of fruit juice. The bold array of colors from the oranges, strawberries, limes, golden mangoes, and papayas makes an effective wake-up call by itself.

The next course is a plate of eggs, cooked in a variety of different ways and accompanied by beans and a chili sauce, which is guaranteed to liven up your taste buds. This dish is usually eaten with warm tortillas (the traditional flattened corn bread) or a crusty *bolillo* (petit pain) and beans. A selection of sweet rolls, coffee, and hot chocolate rounds off the breakfast perfectly. This style of breakfast provides a great start to the day.

Late lunch

As the main meal of the day rarely starts before two o'clock in the afternoon, the benefits of a proper breakfast are fully appreciated by Mexicans. *La comida* (lunch) observes a time-honored formula. The opening course of soup is always followed by a plate of rice, which is treated as a separate serving. Next, there is a main dish of meat or fish, accompanied by vegetables and salad, with beans available as an optional extra. Chili sauce and warm tortillas are on offer throughout the meal. The lunch experience is rounded off with seasonal fruit or a dessert. *Aguas frescas*—fresh fruit beverages—are offered during the meal. They make perfect thirst-quenchers that can be enjoyed at any time of the day.

Light supper

Moving on to the evening, *la cena* (supper) tends to be a light meal served between eight or nine o'clock. Sometimes an *antojito* (snack) is prepared, or some of the lunchtime dishes are reheated. In summer, a crisp salad or fresh fruit medley is sufficient.

Sustaining and special snacks

Especially at weekends or on special occasions, *botanas* (appetizers) are served before a main meal, usually accompanied by a drink. Typical *botanas* include guacamole, fresh cheese, pickled vegetables, and a variety of *antojitos*, such as *tacos*, *quesadillas*, and *tostadas*. *Antojitos* are also perfect when you need to tide over hunger until the next meal and can be enjoyed "on the go," bought from street vendors who offer an impressive range of snacks from their improvised stands. Whatever the time of day in Mexico, you can always be sure of finding something tasty and satisfying to eat!

The Mexican larder

The distinctive qualities of Mexican dishes are provided by a winning combination of flavorsome ingredients, including fresh and dried chilies—some hot and pungent, some mild and sweet; aromatic spices (cinnamon, cumin, cloves, and black pepper); essential herbs such as *epazote*, cilantro, oregano, and thyme; sesame and pumpkin seeds, almonds and other nuts; juicy tomatoes, *tomatillos*, onions, and garlic, sometimes roasted to deepen their flavors; tasty cheeses; and sharp limes and other citrus fruits that give zing and color to a dish. In short, a multitude of healthy and nutritious vegetables, greens, grains, meats, and a remarkable variety of fish and shellfish define the Mexican larder.

Below is a list of some of the main ingredients used in Mexican cooking and featured in the book. Most of them are available from standard supermarkets, while others, such as dried chilies, can be found in specialty and ethnic stores or purchased by mail order or from online suppliers.

AVOCADOS (AGUACATES) Avocados are widely used all over the country in sauces, *antojitos* (snacks), soups, salads, side dishes, and main dishes. It is best to prepare them just before serving, as the flesh begins to darken soon after they are cut, although sprinkling them with lime juice helps to keep them green. Since avocados are rarely sold ripe, buy them a couple of days before they are needed. When ripe, they keep well for a few days in the refrigerator. Of the many varieties of avocado, the Hass avocado, with its knobbly black skin, is one of the most popular around the world. It ripens evenly, peels easily, keeps well, and its flesh is full of flavor.

BEANS (FRIJOLES) Beans, rich in fiber and protein, together with chilies and corn are the staple foods of Mexico. They are important ingredients in many *antojitos*, and make delicious and nutritious soups, side dishes, and main dishes. Freshly cooked beans can be kept for up to a week in the refrigerator and freeze very well. There are many different kinds of beans, varying in size and color from dark black to nearly white. A popular variety is the small black bean, *frijol negro*, mainly used in the south of the country, the Gulf area, and the Yucatan Peninsula. Other popular varieties are the *pinto*, the purplish colored *flor the mayo*, and the pale brown *bayo*, mainly used in central Mexico.

CHEESE (QUESO) There are good melting cheeses, such as *Oaxaca* and *Chihuahua*, used in *antojitos* and main dishes. These can be substituted with Gouda, mozzarella, and mild cheddar. *Queso fresco* is a fresh cheese with a slightly salty taste. It can be eaten by itself as a *botana* (appetizer), as well as cubed or crumbled over *antojitos*, salads, soups, and main dishes. Greek feta cheese is a good substitute. *Queso panela*, a low-salt fresh cheese from central Mexico, is used in *antojitos* such as grilled cheese. An acceptable substitute is buffalo mozzarella.

CHILIES (CHILES) Chilies provide many of the flavors, colors and textures that make Mexican dishes unique. They have an essential oil containing capsaicin, which is thought to be good for the heart and blood circulation and gives chilies their hot, piquant flavor. Chilies are available in Mexico in many different sizes, shapes, and colors, fresh, dried, smoked, or pickled.

Because of their heat, both fresh and dried chilies should be handled with care, preferably using rubber gloves. As a general rule, if you just want to add a very mild chili flavor to a dish, add the whole chili during cooking and discard it before serving. For a slightly hotter, more piquant flavor, cut the chilies in half lengthwise, and remove any seeds and internal veins before adding to the dish. For a strong, full flavor, chop the chili flesh, seeds, and veins and add them all to the dish.

FRESH CHILIES (CHILES FRESCOS) The following are a few of the most popular fresh chilies used frequently in Mexican cooking. *Habanero*, also known as Scotch bonnet, is used mainly in dishes from the Yucatan Peninsula, and is the hottest of all chilies. *Jalapeño*, named after Jalapa, the capital city of the state of Veracruz, is used extensively in salsas and cooked dishes, and is also ideal for pickling. *Poblano* is the largest chili, and can be recognized by its dark green color and pointed tip. It is always cooked before use, with its skin, seeds, and veins removed. It is used extensively in soups and rice, meat, and fish dishes. *Serrano* is a very popular, very hot, thin chili and, like the *jalapeño*, is used in salsas, guacamole, and cooked dishes.

DRIED CHILIES (CHILES SECOS) A wide variety of dried chilies are available, each with its own distinctive flavor and color. They are cooked with other ingredients to make chili sauces and to flavor dishes. They are also used to make two classic Mexican sauces: *Adobo*, a seasoning sauce made with ground dried chilies, herbs, and vinegar, and *Mole*, a cooked sauce made with mainly dried chilies, together with spices, seeds, and sometimes a toasted corn tortilla, fruits, or a piece of chocolate, all finely ground together. Chicken, meat or vegetable stock is also commonly used in its preparation. When buying dried chilies, look for ones that are firm and unbroken. *Ancho*, a dried *poblano* chilli with a dark wrinkly skin, is one of the most popular and mildest dried chili. *Arbol*, a very hot chili with a lovely red color when dried, is used mainly in sauces and casseroles. *Chipotle* is a *jalapeño* that has been dried with warm smoke. It is available dried and either bottled or canned in an *adobo* sauce and gives food a distinctive smoky, slightly sweet flavor. *Guajillo* has an elegant burgundy-red color. A sauce made with this chili will have a rich color and a medium-hot chili flavor. *Mulato* is a dark skinned chili with a medium-hot flavor. *Pasilla* is a long and narrow dried chili with a dark brown color, and its flavor varies from medium-hot to very hot. It is used extensively in *mole* sauces.

CHOCOLATE (CHOCOLATE) Chocolate is made from the seeds of the cacao tree. In Mexico, the cacao beans are ground with sugar and formed into tablets, to which cinnamon, almonds, and vanilla are frequently added. This type of chocolate is used to make drinks and is sometimes added in small amounts to *mole* sauces.

CILANTRO (CILANTRO) This aromatic herb, rich in vitamin B, folic acid, and essential oil, is widely used in Mexican dishes. It gives a distinctive flavor to salsas, soups, salads, and main dishes. It is usually added chopped just before serving.

CINNAMON (CANELA) This popular spice is obtained from the inner bark of the cinnamon tree. It is used in both savory and sweet dishes.

CORN (MAÍZ) Corn is a cereal that remains the main staple in the Mexican diet, and is used both dried and fresh. In the pre-Hispanic era, it was not only the main ingredient to feed the body, but also to feed the soul. In offerings to their gods, native Mexicans always included corn and objects made with it.

Dried corn (*Maíz*) is used to obtain *masa*, the dough from which corn tortillas are made. The dried corn kernels are briefly cooked with lime (calcium oxide) to remove their tough skins and make the cereal easy to digest and increase its nutritional value. The kernels are then ground to a paste, from which the *masa* is obtained. You can make *masa* using *masa harina* (not cornstarch), found in many supermarkets, to make your own tortillas. Alternatively, you can buy them ready-made.

Fresh corn (*Elote*) is a favorite in Mexico. It has a delicate sweet flavor and is a good source of vitamins and minerals. It is popular to eat it whole, either boiled or roasted and seasoned with a half a lime, squeezed and spread over the corn and topped with chili powder. Fresh corn ears are frequently cut into pieces and added to casseroles. Fresh corn kernels are used in soups and vegetable dishes as well as in cakes and breads. Nothing from the corn is

left unused, because even the corn husks are used to wrap food for cooking.

EPAZOTE This highly aromatic, strong-smelling herb is widely used in Mexico to flavor beans, soups, cooked vegetables, and stews. Such is its unique flavor that no other herb can be used as a substitute for epazote. It is available dried from specialty Mexican food suppliers by mail order and online.

NOPALES These are the fleshy oval tender leaves or paddles of the *nopal* cactus, and are very popular mainly in central Mexico. They are cooked and eaten in salads, soups, eggs dishes, and stews. Bottled or canned nopales are an adequate substitute for fresh nopales, but must be thoroughly rinsed before use. Nopales are available from specialty Mexican food stores and suppliers.

PUMPKIN SEEDS (PEPITAS) The seeds of various pumpkins and squashes were highly valued in Mexico long before the arrival of the Spanish. They are eaten roasted and salted as a snack or used ground as a thickening agent in savory dishes.

SESAME SEEDS (AJONJOLÍ) Widely cultivated in Mexico, sesame seeds have a nutty, slightly sweet flavor and are used toasted as a garnish for *mole* sauces and salads. They are also used as a thickening agent for savory dishes.

TOMATILLO Also called the Mexican green tomato, this is a tart-tasting fruit wrapped in a papery husk. It is used either raw or cooked to prepare the most popular Mexican green sauces, such as *salsa verde* and *pipián verde*. Choose firm fruit with a dry, tight-fitting husk, which should be removed before use. Tomatillos can occasionally be found fresh in markets and are also available canned in ethnic stores.

TOMATO (JITOMATE) Ripe fresh tomatoes have been essential to many Mexican dishes since pre-Hispanic times. They are one of the main ingredients of the famous *salsa mexicana* and they are also used raw in salads or cooked in soups, sauces, and casseroles. Many varieties grow in Mexico, but the most commonly used are the round tomato (*jitomate bola*) and the plum tomato (*jitomate guaje*).

Essential equipment

Most of the cooking utensils that were used in Mexico before the arrival of the Spanish are still used for preparing traditional Mexican dishes. The grinding stone and grinding pin (*metate* and *mano*), mortar and pestle (*molcajete* and *mano*), the earthenware griddle (*comal*), wooden chocolate whisk (*molinillo*), and wooden tortilla press (*prensa para tortilla*) can still be seen in action in rural areas in the central part of the country. Even though modern kitchens in the cities have substituted the latest culinary gadgets for some of these native tools, the traditional utensils are still kept on view for purely ornamental purposes.

The most sophisticated meals can be made with the simplest equipment, and you can easily make use of everyday pots, pans, and tools in your kitchen to prepare each of the recipes in this book. The following equipment is recommended:

BLENDER This is one of the most important cooking utensils in the Mexican kitchen. It is necessary for making smooth chili mixtures, soups, and sauces. It is also used to make sorbets, fruit coolers, and Margarita cocktails.

FOOD PROCESSOR This is useful for preparing chunky sauces. It is also important for grinding relatively large quantities of spices and seeds.

MORTAR AND PESTLE This is ideal for grinding small amounts of spices and seeds, and a set should be kept solely for that purpose.

MEDIUM- AND FINE-MESH STRAINERS These are indispensable for straining blended chili mixtures and sauces and separating solids from liquids. A flexible nylon strainer is preferable for using with acidic ingredients, such as raspberries or tomatoes, which may react with the metal and taint or discolor the puree.

HEAVY SAUCEPAN This is excellent for cooking, as it conducts heat efficiently and evenly.

LARGE HEAVY SKILLET This is indispensable for frying or sautéeing food, for even heat distribution over a high heat, and for roasting chilies, tomatoes, onions, and garlic (see page 14), as well as cooking and warming tortillas.

LARGE CAST-IRON STOVE-TOP GRIDDLE PAN This is used for chargrilling meat, fish, or vegetables.

KITCHEN KNIVES A large cook's knife with an 8 inch blade is essential for chopping and slicing, while a small cook's knife with a 4 inch blade is ideal for preparing small ingredients, and a serrated knife is best for cutting tomatoes and fruit.

METAL KITCHEN TONGS These are a must-have for roasting fresh chilies directly over the high flame of a gas burner.

Techniques

Each recipe in this book provides a description of how to prepare the ingredients. However, a more in-depth explanation is given here to highlight some of the key techniques that are used in Mexican cooking, in order to bring out the authentic flavors and textures of the ingredients.

Preparing dried chilies for sauces

Always remove the stems, then tear the chilies open and remove the seeds, as well as all the light-colored veins, in order to give a milder flavor. Roast the chilies in a dry heavy skillet over a medium heat for a few seconds on both sides to bring out their flavors. Then soak them in boiling water for 15–20 minutes until soft, stirring frequently to ensure even soaking. Drain the chilies, transfer to a blender or food processor with some of the soaking liquid and blend until smooth. Reserve or discard the remaining liquid, according to the recipe. Pass the chili mixture through a strainer; this is a very important step, not only to achieve the right texture, but to make the sauces easy to digest. Cook the chili mixture according to the instructions for each recipe.

Roasting fresh chilies

The purpose of roasting chilies, like fresh *poblanos,* is to remove their skins. Roast the whole chilies directly over a high flame of a gas burner or in a dry heavy skillet. Use metal kitchen tongs to keep turning them until the skins are charred and blistered, place the roasted chilies in a plastic bag, wrap the bag in a dish towel and leave for at least 15 minutes—this helps to loosen their skins. Remove the skins and rinse the chilies under cold running water. Slit the chilies lengthwise, discard the stems, seeds, and veins and pat dry.

Roasting tomatoes, onions, and garlic

Roasting vegetables so that they are slightly charred and partly cooked intensifies their flavors. Heat a dry heavy skillet over a medium heat, lay the unpeeled tomatoes, onion, thickly sliced, and whole garlic cloves on the hot surface and roast them, turning occasionally, until soft.

Preparing spices, seeds, and nuts

It is common in Mexico to work with whole spices, almost always toasted and then ground to a dust just before use. Toast the spices in a dry heavy skillet over a medium heat for just a few seconds. This is done not only to intensify their flavor, but also to awaken their aroma. In the same way, seeds and nuts can be toasted for a deeper flavor and then left whole, chopped, or ground as required.

Menu plan

From the mouth-watering selection of snacks, appetizers, main meals, and desserts presented in this book, you can put together a menu to suit every occasion, from simple family meals to dinner parties, barbecues, or Sunday lunches. Whatever the meal, gather your friends and family around the table to share and enjoy this exciting and nutritious food.

LIGHT LUNCH

Baby spinach and mushroom salad (*see page 120*)

Green bean omelet with pasilla chili sauce (*see page 79*)

Quince paste with manchego cheese (*see page 129*)

FAMILY MEAL

Tlalpan-style broth (*see page 42*)

Meatballs in chipotle sauce (*see page 92*)

Mexican-style rice (*see page 40*)

Sweet potato and pineapple dessert (*see page 132*)

FORMAL LUNCH

Duck tacos (*see page 86*)

Seafood casserole (*see page 64*)

White rice (omit the poblano chili strips) (*see page 41*)

Raspberry sorbet (*see page 138*)

WEEKEND BREAKFAST

Hot chocolate (*see page 156*)

Black bean open sandwiches (*see page 26*)

"Rabo de mestiza" poached eggs (*see page 78*)

Fresh fruit gelatin dessert (*see page 134*)

SUNDAY LUNCH

Fish and nopalitos salad (*see page 32*)

Tortilla soup (*see page 54*)

Pork tenderloin in pumpkin seed sauce (*see page 96*)

Crème caramel (*see page 126*)

SUMMER LUNCH PARTY

Guacamole with totopos (*see page 28*)

Green rice with langoustines (*see page 38*)

Beef brochettes with salsa mexicana (*see page 90*)

Nopalitos salad (*see page 116*)

Pickled vegetables (*see page 118*)

Corn cake (*see page 136*)

LARGE GATHERING

Guacamole with totopos (*see page 28*)

Pork pozole casserole with red sauce (*see page 95*)

Mango sorbet (*see page 140*)

Walnut jamoncillo (*see page 133*)

DINNER PARTY

Scallop tostadas (*see page 34*)

Black bean soup (*see page 46*)

Halibut fillets with dried chili sauce (*see page 66*)

White rice (omit the poblano chili strips) (*see page 41*)

Roasted wild berries (*see page 130*)

nd appetizers

Lime-marinated shrimp

Mexico's love affair with shrimp is reflected in the multitude of regional dishes that feature this wonderful shellfish. In this recipe, good-quality shrimp are marinated in freshly squeezed lime juice and enlivened with the kick of chilies.

INGREDIENTS *13 oz cooked peeled shrimp* ‖ *¼ onion, finely chopped* ‖ *3 green chilies, finely chopped (seeded for a milder taste)* ‖ *3 tablespoons freshly squeezed lime juice* ‖ *3 tablespoons extra virgin olive oil* ‖ *a few drops of Worcestershire sauce (optional)* ‖ *1 tablespoon finely chopped fresh cilantro leaves* ‖ *salt and freshly ground black pepper* ‖ *Totopos (see page 28), to serve*

ONE Arrange the shrimp on a chilled serving plate. Sprinkle with the onion and chilies, then drizzle with the lime juice and oil. Sprinkle over the Worcestershire sauce, if using, and season to taste with salt and pepper. Sprinkle the cilantro on top. **TWO** Serve cold with Totopos (see page 28).

Serves 4

NUTRIENT ANALYSIS PER SERVING 780 kJ – 187 cal – 23 g protein – 1 g carbohydrate – 1 g sugars – 10 g fat – 2 g saturated fat – 0 g fiber – 1590 mg sodium

HEALTHY TIP Shrimp are naturally low in saturated fat and also contain a number of essential nutrients such as magnesium, selenium, and zinc. Limes are an excellent source of vitamin C; they are a potent antiseptic and help to fight colds, coughs, and sore throats.

Stuffed jalapeño chilies with tuna

Jalapeño chilies, the dark green chilies from Jalapa, the capital of the east central state of Veracruz, can be hot or very hot and are used all over the country to prepare hot salsas. These famous "stuffed jalapeños" are traditionally prepared in Mexico City during Lent, and make a great snack any time of the year.

INGREDIENTS *12 large jalapeño chilies* ‖ *3 cups water* ‖ *2 tablespoons cider vinegar* ‖ *½ tablespoon salt* ‖ *5 tablespoons brown sugar* ‖ *1 tablespoon olive oil* ‖ *¼ onion, finely chopped* ‖ *1 garlic clove, finely chopped* ‖ *2 tomatoes, skinned, seeded, and chopped* ‖ *7 oz can tuna steak in olive oil, well drained and flaked* ‖ *1 bay leaf* ‖ *5 green olives, pitted and chopped* ‖ *1 teaspoon chopped flat leaf parsley leaves* ‖ *salt and freshly ground black pepper*

ONE Wearing rubber gloves (to avoid irritating your skin), use a sharp knife to make a vertical slit down the length of each chili and carefully remove the seeds and veins. **TWO** Put the measured water in a large saucepan with the vinegar, salt, and sugar and bring to a boil. Add the chilies and boil for 5 minutes. Remove the pan from the heat, drain the chilies and transfer to a bowl of fresh cold water. **THREE** Heat the oil in a heavy saucepan over a medium heat and sauté the onion until soft. Add the garlic and sauté for an additional minute. Add the tomatoes and simmer gently for about 5 minutes, stirring constantly. Add the tuna, bay leaf, olives, and parsley, and season to taste with salt and pepper. Simmer for about 10 minutes until the mixture thickens and looks dry. Allow to cool. **FOUR** Drain the chilies well and pat dry. Carefully stuff with the tuna mixture. Arrange the stuffed chilies on a plate and serve at room temperature.

Serves 4

NUTRIENT ANALYSIS PER SERVING 978 kJ – 230 cal – 18 g protein – 23 g carbohydrate – 22 g sugars – 9 g fat – 1 g saturated fat – 1 g fiber – 490 mg sodium

HEALTHY TIP Chilies are an excellent source of the powerful antioxidant vitamin C. They also provide minerals including molybdenum, manganese, phosphorus, potassium, thiamine, and copper. They stimulate the appetite and digestive system, and are good for the heart and circulation. Tuna is rich in vitamin D and omega-3 fatty acids—excellent for the cardiovascular system.

Mushroom quesadillas

Quesadillas are a typical *antojito*—an informal savory snack served before the main meal. They consist of corn tortillas filled with a variety of ingredients, such as cheese, sautéed mushrooms, potatoes with chorizo or shredded meat, to mention but a few. Folded over half-moon-style, they can be pan-fried in a little oil or cooked in a dry skillet, as in this recipe.

INGREDIENTS *2 tablespoons olive oil* ‖ *1 onion, finely chopped* ‖ *2 green chilies, finely chopped* ‖ *2 garlic cloves, crushed* ‖ *1 lb mushrooms, a mixture of wild and cultivated, roughly chopped* ‖ *1 teaspoon lime juice* ‖ *1 teaspoon finely chopped fresh epazote (if available) or 1 tablespoon finely chopped flat leaf parsley* ‖ *8 soft corn tortillas* ‖ *salt and freshly ground black pepper*

ONE Heat the oil in a heavy skillet over a gentle heat and sauté the onions until soft. **TWO** Add the chilies and garlic and sauté for 1 minute. Add the mushrooms and sauté for a few seconds over a medium-high heat. Add the lime juice and epazote or parsley, season to taste with salt and pepper and cook for an additional 5 minutes, or until the mushrooms are just cooked. **THREE** Preheat a large, dry heavy skillet over a medium heat. Warm each side of the tortillas, 2–3 at a time, in the hot pan for about 30 seconds until soft. Place some of the mushroom mixture on one half of each tortilla, then fold over the other half, pressing it down for a few seconds. Turn over and cook until the tortillas become slightly crisp. Transfer to a warm platter and cover with a clean dish towel while you repeat with the remaining tortillas and filling. Serve immediately.

Serves 4

NUTRIENT ANALYSIS PER SERVING 1425 kJ – 339 cal – 11 g protein – 48 g carbohydrate – 2 g sugars – 12 g fat – 1 g saturated fat – 6 g fiber – 220 mg sodium

HEALTHY TIP Mushrooms are an excellent source of minerals such as selenium, copper, potassium, phosphorus, and zinc. They are also a good source of B-complex vitamins.

Black bean open sandwiches

Beans are a very important source of protein in the Mexican diet. They are prepared in many different ways and served at any time of the day. *Molletes* such as these—open crusty bread rolls filled with refried beans topped with melted cheese—are often served for breakfast or a light dinner in Mexico City cafeterias, usually accompanied by salsa mexicana.

INGREDIENTS *4 crusty bread rolls or 8 slices French bread* ‖ *1½ tablespoons unsalted butter* ‖ *½ cup grated mild cheddar cheese* ‖ *Salsa Mexicana (see page 90), to serve* ‖ *finely chopped red chili, to garnish (optional)* ‖ *finely chopped cilantro, to garnish (optional)*

REFRIED BEANS *1¼ cups dried black beans* ‖ *6 cups cold water* ‖ *1 small onion, halved* ‖ *2 garlic cloves, peeled* ‖ *1 fresh epazote sprig (if available)* ‖ *½ teaspoon salt* ‖ *2 tablespoons vegetable oil*

ONE First make the refried beans. Put the beans in a large saucepan, add cold water to cover by 5–6 inches and allow to soak overnight (8–12 hours). **TWO** Drain the beans, rinse, and cover with the measured cold water. Add the onion, garlic cloves, and epazote sprig. Bring to a boil, then reduce the heat and simmer, partially covered, for 2–3 hours until the beans are soft. Check frequently: if the beans appear above the water level during the cooking time, add boiling water (never use cold water) to cover. **THREE** Remove the onion, garlic, and epazote and add the salt. Drain the beans and puree in a blender or food processor, or mash with a potato masher while still warm. Heat the oil in a heavy saucepan over a medium heat, add the beans and cook until dry, stirring constantly. Remove from the heat and allow to cool—the bean puree will thicken. **FOUR** Cut the bread rolls in half horizontally and remove some of the soft inside crumb. Spread with the butter, add the refried beans on top and sprinkle with the cheese. Place on a baking sheet and bake in a preheated oven, 350°F, for 6–8 minutes until the cheese has melted and the bread is lightly toasted. **FIVE** Scatter over the chili and cilantro, if desired, then serve hot with Salsa Mexicana (see page 90).

Serves 4

NUTRIENT ANALYSIS PER SERVING 1890 kJ – 448 cal – 23 g protein – 57 g carbohydrate – 3 g sugars – 16 g fat – 6 g saturated fat – 17 g fiber – 660 mg sodium

HEALTHY TIP Well known for their high nutritional value, black beans are a very good source of protein, carbohydrates, calcium, iron, manganese, and phosphorus, as well as many other minerals and vitamins. They are also an excellent source of dietary fiber and amino acids.

Guacamole with chips
Crisp and lightly salted *totopos* are fried corn tortilla triangles usually served to accompany refried beans or guacamole, the ever-popular avocado salsa flavored with green chilies, onions, and cilantro. This Mexican specialty is prepared all over the country and can be served as a side dish to grilled meats, salads, and rice or simply spooned over any kind of taco.

INGREDIENTS *2 large ripe avocados* ‖ *1 tablespoon finely chopped onion* ‖ *2 serrano or jalapeño chilies, finely chopped* ‖ *2 tablespoons finely chopped cilantro leaves, plus extra leaves to garnish* ‖ *a few drops of freshly squeezed lime juice* ‖ *salt*
CHIPS *6 soft corn tortillas* ‖ *vegetable oil, for brushing* ‖ *salt*

ONE To make the chips, brush each side of the tortillas with a little oil and cut into triangles. Arrange on a baking sheet and bake in a preheated oven, 350°F, for 8–10 minutes until crisp. Sprinkle with a little salt and allow to cool on a wire rack. **TWO** Halve the avocados and remove the pits. Cut the flesh into ½ inch cubes, then use a spoon to scoop out the remaining flesh from the skin and put in a bowl. **THREE** Add the onion, chilies, and cilantro to the bowl and mix together gently, making sure that you don't squash the avocado. Add the lime juice and season to taste with salt. Garnish with cilantro leaves and serve immediately with the chips.

Serves 4

NUTRIENT ANALYSIS PER SERVING 1607 kJ – 385 cal – 8 g protein – 37 g carbohydrate – 1 g sugars – 23 g fat – 4 g saturated fat – 2 g fiber – 167 mg sodium

HEALTHY TIP Avocados contain a wide variety of nutrients including vitamins and minerals, as well as heart-healthy monounsaturated fat. High in vitamin E, they are easily digested and help to prevent anemia. Cilantro has antibiotic properties and helps to relieve digestive problems.

Jumbo shrimp taquitos

Tacos, a favorite Mexican *antojito* (snack), are filled and rolled-up soft corn tortillas. There are no limits to the type of fillings and they vary according to the region, but they are usually served with a hot chili sauce. These mouth-watering shrimp *taquitos* are traditionally served in Baja California and the states of the northern Pacific Coast.

INGREDIENTS *2 tablespoons olive oil* ‖ *1 onion, thinly sliced lengthwise* ‖ *1 lb uncooked jumbo shrimp, peeled and deveined* ‖ *2 garlic cloves, crushed* ‖ *4 serrano chilies, seeded and sliced into thin strips* ‖ *1 tablespoon chopped cilantro* ‖ *8 soft corn tortillas* ‖ *salt and freshly ground black pepper* ‖ *Guacamole (see page 28) or your favorite salsa, to serve* ‖ *cilantro, to garnish*

ONE Heat the oil in a skillet over a gentle heat and sauté the onion for 1 minute. **TWO** Add the shrimp, garlic, and chilies and sauté for about 3 minutes—the shrimp are cooked when they turn pink and curl up. Season to taste with salt and pepper and sprinkle the cilantro on top. Keep warm. **THREE** Preheat a large, dry heavy skillet over a medium heat. Warm each side of the tortillas, 2–3 at a time, in the hot pan for about 30 seconds until soft. Place some of the shrimp mixture in the center of each tortilla and roll up. Transfer to a warm platter and cover with a clean dish towel while you repeat with the remaining tortillas and shrimp mixture. **FOUR** Serve immediately with Guacamole (see page 28) or your favorite salsa, garnished with cilantro.

Serves 4

NUTRIENT ANALYSIS PER SERVING 1750 kJ – 416 cal – 30 g protein – 47 g carbohydrate – 1 g sugars – 12 g fat – 1 g saturated fat – 3 g fiber – 480 mg sodium

HEALTHY TIP Shrimp are a good source of protein, highly nutritious and easy to digest. Chilies contain vitamin C and capsaicin, and are recommended for circulatory and digestive problems.

Fish and nopalitos salad

This is a typical Mexican appetizer made with marinated fish and inspired by the traditional recipe of ceviche from Zihuatanejo in the state of Guerrero on the Pacific Coast. The nopales, the fleshy oval leaves of the nopal cactus, add a delicate texture and slightly tart flavor.

INGREDIENTS *12 cod or sole fillets, skinned, rinsed, and patted dry* ‖ *2 red chilies, seeded and finely sliced* ‖ *2 green chilies, seeded and finely sliced* ‖ *1 red onion, finely sliced lengthwise* ‖ *6 tablespoons freshly squeezed lime juice* ‖ *7 oz cooked fresh nopales, cut into strips* ‖ *4 radishes, finely sliced* ‖ *salt and freshly ground black pepper* ‖ *cilantro leaves, to garnish* ‖ *Totopos (see page 28), to serve*

DRESSING *4 tablespoons extra virgin olive oil* ‖ *1½ tablespoons freshly squeezed lime juice, or to taste* ‖ *½ teaspoon honey* ‖ *½ teaspoon dried oregano* ‖ *salt*

ONE Cut the fish into ½ x 1½ inch strips. Put in a glass bowl with the chilies and onion. Add the lime juice and season with salt and pepper. Cover and allow to marinate in the refrigerator for 1 hour. **TWO** Drain the excess lime juice and add the nopales and radishes. Mix all the dressing ingredients together well and pour over the fish mixture. Check the seasoning. **THREE** To serve, divide the fish and nopalitos salad between 4 plates. Garnish with cilantro leaves and add a couple of Totopos (see page 28) on the side of each serving.

Serves 4

NUTRIENT ANALYSIS PER SERVING 825 kJ – 198 cal – 17 g protein – 6 g carbohydrate – 4 g sugars – 12 g fat – 2 g saturated fat – 2 g fiber – 80 mg sodium

HEALTHY TIP An excellent source of vitamin A and C, nopales are also a good source of the B vitamins and calcium. Cod is a good source of vitamins B6 and 12, and is also beneficial for cardiovascular health. (If possible, try to use cod from sustainable sources or farmed cod.) Sole is a good source of selenium, potassium, and vitamins B6 and B12.

Scallop tostadas

A delicate and tasty starter made with fresh scallops placed on a tostada, a crunchy corn tortilla. A tostada is a typical *antojito* (snack), popular throughout Mexico. It can be either eaten plain or topped with fresh ingredients that vary according to the region.

INGREDIENTS *7 oz uncooked scallops, white flesh only ‖ ¼ red onion, finely sliced ‖ 2 jalapeño chilies, seeded and finely sliced ‖ 4 inch piece of cucumber, seeded and cut into cubes ‖ 2 teaspoons finely chopped chives ‖ 2 tablespoons freshly squeezed lime juice ‖ 2 tablespoons extra virgin olive oil ‖ 4 soft corn tortillas, preferably small ‖ salt and freshly ground black pepper*

TO GARNISH *cilantro leaves ‖ lime wedges*

ONE Slice each scallop into 3–4 equal pieces about ¼ inch thick and place in a glass bowl. Add the red onion, chilies, cucumber, and chives. Gently stir and mix with the lime juice and oil. Season to taste with salt and pepper. Cover and allow to marinate in the refrigerator for 20 minutes. **TWO** If you cannot find small corn tortillas, use a 4–5 inch round cookie cutter to cut out rounds from large corn tortillas. Place the tortillas on a baking sheet and bake in a preheated oven, 350°F, for 8–10 minutes until crisp. Leave to cool before using. **THREE** Assemble the tostadas just before serving. Using a slotted spoon, place a quarter of the scallop mixture on top of each tostada. Garnish with cilantro leaves and lime wedges and serve immediately.

Serves 4

NUTRIENT ANALYSIS PER SERVING (using small tortillas or cut small rounds, weighing approximately ½ oz each) 727 kJ – 173 cal – 14 g protein – 13 g carbohydrate – 1 g sugars – 8 g fat – 1 g saturated fat – 1 g fiber – 139 mg sodium

HEALTHY TIP Crisping the tortillas in the oven rather than deep-frying them, as is traditionally the cooking method, makes these tostadas even healthier.

Soups and rice

Green rice with langoustines

The combination of rice and shellfish is much loved in Mexico. Here, fragrant basmati rice is colored green with cilantro and spinach, seasoned with a poblano chili and served with langoustines to offer a delicious combination of flavors and textures.

INGREDIENTS *1 ½ cups basmati rice ‖ 1 poblano chili ‖ ¼ cup cilantro ‖ ½ cup spinach ‖ ¼ onion ‖ 1 garlic clove ‖ 2 cups chicken stock ‖ 2 tablespoons vegetable oil ‖ 3 garlic cloves, crushed ‖ 1 tablespoon olive oil ‖ 8 uncooked langoustines, in their shells, legs removed, or 8 uncooked large jumbo shrimp, in their shells, deveined and legs removed ‖ salt and freshly ground black pepper*

ONE Soak the rice in hot water for 15 minutes. Drain, rinse well, and drain again. **TWO** Carefully hold the chili over a high gas flame with metal kitchen tongs or put in a preheated dry heavy skillet over a high heat, turning frequently, until the skin is charred. Put the roasted chili in a plastic bag, wrap the bag with a dish towel and allow to sweat for at least 15 minutes. Remove the skin, discard the stem and seeds, rinse and pat dry. **THREE** Put the chili, cilantro, spinach, onion, and whole garlic in a blender or food processor and blend to a fairly smooth texture. **FOUR** Cook the mixture in a heavy saucepan over a medium heat for about 8 minutes, stirring constantly. Add the stock, bring to a boil and season to taste with salt. Keep warm. **FIVE** Heat the vegetable oil in a heavy saucepan over a medium heat and sauté the rice, stirring constantly, for about 5 minutes, or until it loses its stickiness. Add the chili and stock mixture and bring to a boil, stirring. Reduce the heat to low, cover and cook for about 10 minutes, or until the liquid has been absorbed and the rice is tender. Remove from the heat and allow to rest for 10 minutes. **SIX** Mix the crushed garlic, olive oil, and a little salt together to make a paste. Heat a wok or a heavy skillet over a high heat and sauté the langoustines or jumbo shrimp with the garlic paste for a few minutes. Turn the langoustines or shrimp over and cook on the other side for an additional minute until cooked through. **SEVEN** Transfer the rice to a warm platter and arrange the langoustines on top. Season to taste with pepper and serve immediately.

Serves 4

NUTRIENT ANALYSIS PER SERVING 1643 kJ – 394 cal – 11 g protein – 67 g carbohydrate – 1 g sugars – 9 g fat – 1 g saturated fat – 2 g fiber – 253 mg sodium

HEALTHY TIP Langoustines are highly nutritious and easy to digest. They are an excellent source of protein as well as selenium, an antioxidant that protects from heart disease and is vital for a healthy immune system.

Tlalpan-style broth

Soups are an integral part of the Mexican diet. In central Mexico, lunch generally starts with a soup followed by rice and a main course with vegetables. This broth contains a healthy combination of chicken, chickpeas, carrots, and avocado, which marries beautifully with the smoky chipotle chili.

INGREDIENTS *6 cups chicken stock ‖ 6 oz boneless, skinless chicken breast ‖ 1 tablespoon vegetable oil ‖ 1 onion, finely chopped ‖ 2 carrots, peeled and diced ‖ 2 garlic cloves, finely chopped ‖ 2⅓ cups cooked chickpeas ‖ 1 chipotle chili, bottled or canned in adobo sauce, seeded and cut into strips ‖ 1 large ripe avocado, pitted, peeled, and diced ‖ 2 tablespoons chopped cilantro ‖ salt ‖ 1 lime, cut into wedges, to serve*

ONE Put the stock and chicken in a saucepan and bring to a boil. Reduce the heat to medium and simmer for about 20 minutes until the chicken is cooked. Remove the chicken from the stock, reserving the stock, and allow to cool. Shred the chicken and set aside. **TWO** Heat the oil in a large saucepan over a medium heat and sauté the onion and carrots until the onion is translucent. Add the garlic and cook for an additional minute. Pour in the reserved stock and simmer for 10 minutes. Add the chickpeas and simmer for an additional 10 minutes. Season to taste with salt. **THREE** Just before serving, add the chili and shredded chicken to the broth and heat through. Pour the broth into warm bowls and sprinkle with the avocado and cilantro. Serve with the lime wedges on the side.

Serves 4

NUTRIENT ANALYSIS PER SERVING 1354 kJ – 324 cal – 20 g protein – 25 g carbohydrate – 6 g sugars – 16 g fat – 3 g saturated fat – 7 g fiber – 257 mg sodium

HEALTHY TIP This is a highly nutritious chicken and vegetable soup. To mention just a few of the health benefits, chickpeas are an excellent source of complex carbohydrates and dietary fiber. They also provide protein, vitamins, and minerals such as calcium, potassium, and iron, as well as having antiseptic and diuretic properties.

Black bean soup

Beans are a staple ingredient of Mexican cuisine and are served as starters, soups, salads, or as a main dish. Black bean soup is a great favorite, especially when topped with fried tortilla strips and garnished with crumbled white cheese. Here, a hint of dried oregano has been added to enhance the delicious flavor.

INGREDIENTS *1¼ cups dried black beans* ‖ *6 cups cold water* ‖ *1 small onion, halved, and ½ onion, chopped* ‖ *4 garlic cloves, peeled* ‖ *1 fresh epazote sprig (if available)* ‖ *1 teaspoon salt* ‖ *2 cups vegetable or chicken stock* ‖ *2 tomatoes, skinned and seeded* ‖ *1 tablespoon olive oil* ‖ *vegetable oil, for brushing* ‖ *2 soft corn tortillas* ‖ *4 oz feta cheese, diced* ‖ *1 red chili, seeded and finely sliced* ‖ *dried oregano, for sprinkling*

ONE Soak the beans in plenty of cold water for 8–12 hours. **TWO** Drain the beans, rinse, and cover with the measured cold water. Add the halved onion, 2 of the garlic cloves, and the epazote sprig. Bring to a boil, then reduce the heat and simmer, partially covered, for 2–3 hours until the beans are soft. If the beans appear above the water level during the cooking time, add boiling water (never cold water) to cover. **THREE** Remove the onion, garlic, and epazote and add the salt. Puree the beans with their cooking water and half of the stock in a blender or food processor, then sieve. Add more stock if the mixture is too thick. **FOUR** Puree the tomatoes with the remaining garlic cloves and the chopped onion in the blender or food processor. Heat the olive oil in a heavy saucepan, add the tomato mixture and simmer for 5–8 minutes, stirring constantly. Add the bean mixture and simmer for 10 minutes. Check the seasoning. **FIVE** Brush each side of the tortillas with a little vegetable oil, then cut into thin strips. Spread out on a baking sheet and bake in a preheated oven, 350°F, for 6–8 minutes until golden. **SIX** Serve the soup in individual bowls, topped with a few tortilla strips. Scatter over the feta and chili, and sprinkle the oregano on the top.

Serves 4

NUTRIENT ANALYSIS PER SERVING 1463 kJ – 347 cal – 21 g protein – 45 g carbohydrate – 6 g sugars – 11 g fat – 4 g saturated fat – 16 g fiber – 1126 mg sodium

HEALTHY TIP Black beans are a very good source of cholesterol-lowering fiber. They also prevent blood sugar levels from rising too rapidly after a meal, great for individuals with diabetes or hypoglycemia.

Milpa soup

Milpa is the term for a corn field where a great variety of vegetables and fruit are also cultivated. This soup is one of the pre-Hispanic dishes that use vegetables harvested in the *milpa*, such as corn, zucchini, poblano chilies, and green beans, and is flavored with the herb epazote.

INGREDIENTS *2 poblano chilies* ‖ *1 tablespoon vegetable oil* ‖ *½ onion, finely chopped* ‖ *1 garlic clove, finely chopped* ‖ *1 ½ cups fresh corn kernels* ‖ *2 zucchini, cut into small strips* ‖ *4 oz green beans, cut into pieces* ‖ *4 cups chicken stock* ‖ *2 large fresh epazote sprigs (if available) or fresh cilantro sprigs* ‖ *salt and freshly ground black pepper*

ONE Carefully hold the chilies over a high gas flame with metal kitchen tongs or put in a preheated dry heavy skillet over a high heat, turning frequently, until the skins are charred. Put the roasted chilies in a plastic bag, wrap the bag with a dish towel and allow to sweat for at least 15 minutes. Remove the skins, rinse the chilies under cold running water and discard the stems and seeds. Pat dry and slice lengthwise into strips. **TWO** Heat the oil in a large saucepan over a medium heat and sauté the onion until soft. Add the chilies, garlic, and the remaining vegetables and sauté for about 3 minutes, stirring constantly. **THREE** Add the stock and bring to a boil. Add the epazote or cilantro sprigs, reduce the heat and simmer gently for about 10 minutes until the vegetables are cooked. Season to taste with salt and pepper. **FOUR** Discard the epazote, if using, and serve the soup hot in bowls.

Serves 4

NUTRIENT ANALYSIS PER SERVING 458 kJ – 109 cal – 4 g protein – 14 g carbohydrate – 4 g sugars – 5 g fat – 1 g saturated fat – 3 g fiber – 208 mg sodium

HEALTHY TIP This delicious and nutritious vegetable soup is packed with vitamins, minerals, and other nutrients that help to strengthen the immune system. In addition, the vegetables are a good source of dietary fiber.

Chilled avocado soup

Avocados were consumed by the inhabitants of southern Mexico and Central America before the arrival of the Spanish. They were easily accepted in Europe mainly because of their reputation as an aphrodisiac. This delicious and refreshing soup is ideal for a hot summer's day.

INGREDIENTS *2 large ripe avocados, pitted and peeled* ‖ *1 teaspoon freshly squeezed lime juice* ‖ *4 cups fresh chicken stock, chilled and solidified fat removed* ‖ *1 teaspoon chopped cilantro, plus extra to garnish* ‖ *salt and freshly ground black pepper*

ONE Put the avocados, lime juice, about half the stock, and the cilantro in a blender or food processor and blend until smooth. **TWO** Pour the avocado mixture into a glass bowl. Add the remaining stock, mix thoroughly and season to taste with salt and pepper. Cover and chill in the refrigerator. **THREE** Serve in individual soup bowls, sprinkled with chopped cilantro to garnish.

Serves 4

NUTRIENT ANALYSIS PER SERVING 778 kJ – 189 cal – 2 g protein – 2 g carbohydrate – 1 g sugars – 19 g fat – 4 g saturated fat – 0 g fiber – 210 mg sodium

HEALTHY TIP Most of the fats in avocados are health-promoting monounsaturated fats, especially oleic acid. Avocados are rich in vitamin E, which protects cells against the harmful effects of toxins. They also contain a fair amount of vitamin C, thiamine, riboflavin, and potassium, the latter a mineral that helps to regulate blood pressure.

Carrot and beet soup

A glorious soup made from two humble root vegetables. The color is in itself a feast for the eyes.

INGREDIENTS *1 tablespoon olive oil* ‖ *12 oz carrots, roughly chopped* ‖ *1 large onion, roughly chopped* ‖ *1 leek, white part only, roughly chopped* ‖ *1 garlic clove, crushed* ‖ *5 cups vegetable or chicken stock* ‖ *4 oz beet, cooked and roughly chopped* ‖ *3 oz feta cheese, crumbled* ‖ *2 tablespoons finely chopped cilantro* ‖ *salt and freshly ground black pepper* ‖ *griddled corn tortillas, to serve (optional)*

ONE Heat the oil in a large heavy saucepan over a gentle heat. Add the carrots, onion, and leek, cover and gently sweat for 10 minutes, stirring occasionally. **TWO** Add the garlic and stock and bring to a boil, then reduce the heat and simmer for 20–25 minutes until the carrots are just tender. Allow to cool. **THREE** Transfer to a blender or food processor, add the beet and blend until smooth. Return to the saucepan, reheat and season to taste with salt and pepper. **FOUR** Serve in individual bowls, sprinkled with the feta and cilantro, with corn tortillas to accompany, if desired.

Serves 4–6

NUTRIENT ANALYSIS PER SERVING 579 kJ – 139 cal – 5 g protein – 14 g carbohydrate – 12 g sugars – 7 g fat – 3 g saturated fat – 5 g fiber – 518 mg sodium

HEALTHY TIP Carrots and beets are packed with healthy nutrients and are an excellent source of vitamin A and potassium. These two super vegetables are well known for their medicinal properties and for the support they give to the immune system.

Tortilla soup

Also known as "Aztec soup," this is one of the most delicious and typical soups of central Mexico. The broth is seasoned with the aromatic herb epazote, native to Mesoamerica, which gives a distinctive flavor to the soup. It is typically garnished with cheese, avocado, and pasilla chili rings.

INGREDIENTS *2 medium-large ripe tomatoes, skinned and seeded* ‖ *1 garlic clove, roughly chopped* ‖ *½ onion, roughly chopped* ‖ *1 tablespoon vegetable oil, plus extra for brushing and frying* ‖ *6 cups chicken stock* ‖ *3 large fresh epazote sprigs (if available) or fresh cilantro sprigs* ‖ *8 soft corn tortillas* ‖ *2 pasilla chilies* ‖ *4 oz feta cheese, diced* ‖ *1 large ripe avocado, pitted, peeled, and diced* ‖ *salt and freshly ground black pepper*

ONE Puree the tomatoes in a blender or food processor with the garlic and onion, adding a small amount of the stock if too thick. **TWO** Heat the oil in a large saucepan over a medium heat, add the tomato mixture and cook for 2 minutes. Reduce the heat and simmer gently for about 8 minutes until cooked, stirring constantly. **THREE** Add the stock and bring to a boil. Add the epazote or cilantro sprigs, reduce the heat and simmer for about 15 minutes. Discard the epazote or cilantro sprigs and season to taste with salt and pepper. **FOUR** Brush both sides of each tortilla with a little oil and cut into thin strips. Spread out on a baking sheet and bake in a preheated oven, 350°F, for 8–10 minutes until golden brown. **FIVE** Meanwhile, cut the chilies into ¼ inch rings, discarding the seeds. Heat a little oil in a small skillet and fry the chili rings for about 10 seconds, or until crisp. Drain on paper towels. **SIX** To serve, place an equal quantity of the tortilla strips in the center of each soup plate, scatter over the feta, avocado, and a few chili rings, then pour over the very hot soup.

Serves 4

NUTRIENT ANALYSIS PER SERVING 2019 kJ – 483 cal – 13 g protein – 50 g carbohydrate – 3 g sugars – 26 g fat – 6 g saturated fat – 3 g fiber – 786 mg sodium

HEALTHY TIP This nutritious soup is suitable for people with gluten intolerance, if the tortillas are pure corn (some bought soft corn tortillas may contain wheat gluten), and contains health-promoting tomatoes and avocados, which are rich in vitamins and minerals, and good sources of dietary fiber. They can also help guard against certain cancers and sustain energy levels.

Tuna steaks with salsa arriera

There is nothing like a delicious salsa to enhance the magnificent flavor of a seared tuna steak. Traditionally, *salsa arriera* is extremely hot, prepared with chopped onions and chilies marinated in lime juice with a hint of oregano, but there is always the option of making it milder by using fewer chilies and removing their seeds.

INGREDIENTS *4 x 6 oz fresh tuna steaks ‖ 1 tablespoon olive oil ‖ 1 garlic clove, crushed ‖ salt and freshly ground black pepper ‖ lime wedges, or snipped chives, to garnish*

SALSA ARRIERA *1 onion, finely chopped ‖ 6 tablespoons freshly squeezed lime juice ‖ 4–5 green chilies, finely chopped (seeded for a milder taste) ‖ 1 teaspoon dried oregano, or to taste ‖ salt and freshly ground black pepper*

ONE Brush the tuna steaks with the oil and garlic and season with salt and pepper. Cover and chill in the refrigerator for at least 20 minutes. **TWO** Meanwhile, mix all the salsa ingredients together in a glass bowl and allow to stand at room temperature for at least 15 minutes. Check the seasoning. **THREE** Preheat a ridged stove-top griddle pan over a medium-high heat. Add the tuna steaks to the hot pan and cook for 2–3 minutes on each side until cooked—they should be opaque, lightly browned, and firm, but still moist. **FOUR** Transfer the tuna steaks to a warm dish and spoon the salsa on top. Serve immediately with lime wedges or garnish with snipped chives.

Serves 4

NUTRIENT ANALYSIS PER SERVING 1185 kJ – 280 cal – 43 g protein – 3 g carbohydrate – 2 g sugars – 11 g fat – 3 g saturated fat – 0 g fiber – 85 mg sodium

HEALTHY TIP An excellent source of high-quality protein, tuna is rich in a variety of important nutrients, including the minerals selenium, magnesium, and potassium; the B vitamins niacin, B1, and B6; and perhaps, most importantly, the beneficial omega-3 essential fatty acids. The salsa ingredients are outstanding foods for maintaining the immune system.

Red snapper Veracruz-style
This is one of the most popular dishes in Mexico, traditionally made with red snapper, but equally good with any white fish. The sauce, of international acclaim, is the result of a combination of ingredients from two cultures—pre-Hispanic Mexico and Spain.

INGREDIENTS *4 x 6 oz red snapper fillets or white fish fillets, cleaned ‖ 1 tablespoon freshly squeezed lime juice ‖ 1 tablespoon olive oil ‖ 1 onion, finely chopped ‖ 2 garlic cloves, finely chopped ‖ 8 large plum tomatoes, skinned, seeded, and finely chopped ‖ 1 jalapeño chili, deseeded and finely sliced ‖ 16 green olives, pitted and sliced ‖ 1 tablespoon capers ‖ 1 bay leaf ‖ pinch of dried oregano ‖ 4 Spanish yellow peppers in brine, drained (if available) ‖ salt and freshly ground black pepper ‖ flat leaf parsley sprigs, to garnish*

ONE Place the fish fillets in a glass bowl. Sprinkle them with the lime juice and season with salt and pepper. Cover and allow to marinate in the refrigerator for 30–45 minutes. **TWO** Heat the oil in a heavy skillet over a medium heat and sauté the onion for about 7 minutes, until soft. Add the garlic and sauté for about another minute. Add the tomatoes, chili, olives, capers, bay leaf, and oregano and bring to a boil. Reduce the heat and simmer for about 20 minutes, stirring constantly. Season to taste with salt and pepper and allow to cool completely. **THREE** Place the fish fillets in the cold sauce, making sure that the fish is well covered with the sauce. Cover and cook over a low heat for about 6–8 minutes, or until the fish is cooked through. **FOUR** Serve immediately, garnished with the Spanish yellow peppers, if using, and parsley sprigs.

Serves 4

NUTRIENT ANALYSIS PER SERVING 1100 kJ – 264 cal – 35 g protein – 10 g carbohydrate – 9 g sugars – 9 g fat – 1 g saturated fat – 4 g fiber – 560 mg sodium

HEALTHY TIP This sauce contains healthy ingredients such as tomatoes, rich in vitamins A and C, and olives, believed to reduce the risk of cardiovascular disease. Olives contain several important vitamins and minerals including vitamins A and E, phosphorus, potassium, and manganese.

Seafood casserole

With the thousands of miles of coastline surrounding the country, Mexico offers a great variety of delicious fish and shellfish in abundance. You can enjoy them in the different types of regional dishes, which vary according to the customs and the local ingredients. This recipe features an enticing, nutritious mixture, cooked in a fresh tomato sauce.

INGREDIENTS *4 tablespoons olive oil ‖ ½ onion, finely chopped ‖ 4 garlic cloves, crushed ‖ 2 lb tomatoes, skinned, seeded, and chopped ‖ 1 bay leaf ‖ 10 oz uncooked large jumbo shrimp, peeled and deveined ‖ 10 oz uncooked scallops, white part only ‖ 10 oz halibut fillet, cut into bite-size cubes ‖ 10 oz uncooked squid, cleaned and cut into thin rings ‖ 10 oz cooked octopus, cut into 1¼ inch pieces ‖ 1 tablespoon finely chopped flat leaf parsley ‖ salt and freshly ground black pepper ‖ plain White Rice (see page 41—omit the Poblano Chili Strips), to serve*

ONE Heat 2 tablespoons of the oil in a heavy saucepan over a medium heat and sauté the onion until soft. Add the garlic and sauté for an additional minute. Add the tomatoes and bay leaf and bring to a boil. Reduce the heat and simmer gently for about 20 minutes, stirring constantly. Season to taste with salt and pepper. If the sauce is very thick, add a little water. Keep hot. **TWO** Heat the remaining oil in a wok or a large heavy skillet. Add the shrimp, scallops, halibut, squid, and octopus, season with salt and pepper and sauté over a high heat for 2–3 minutes. Add the hot sauce and bring to a boil briefly. Check the seasoning. **THREE** Transfer to a hot serving platter and sprinkle the parsley on top. Serve immediately with the plain White Rice (see page 41).

Serves 4

NUTRIENT ANALYSIS PER SERVING 1876 kJ – 445 cal – 61 g protein – 13 g carbohydrate – 8 g sugars – 17 g fat – 3 g saturated fat – 4 g fiber – 754 mg sodium

HEALTHY TIP Shellfish are an excellent source of protein; they are low in fat and rich in essential minerals such as zinc, selenium, and copper. They also are a good source of vitamin B12 and niacin.

Rainbow trout in papillotte

In this dish, rainbow trout are rubbed with lime juice and stuffed with a mixture of onion, chili, garlic, and fresh cilantro, where the chilies give a really distinctive edge, creating a harmony of flavors and textures.

INGREDIENTS *4 rainbow trout, cleaned and gutted* ‖ *2 tablespoons freshly squeezed lime juice* ‖ *salt and freshly ground black pepper* ‖ *1 tablespoon olive oil, plus extra for brushing and oiling* ‖ *½ onion, finely chopped* ‖ *2 garlic cloves, finely chopped* ‖ *2 green chilies, finely sliced* ‖ *2 red chilies, finely sliced* ‖ *large bunch of cilantro, chopped*

ONE Rinse the fish and pat dry. With a sharp knife, cut 3 diagonal slashes in the sides of each fish. Rub the fish inside and out with the lime juice and season with salt and pepper. **TWO** Heat the oil in a skillet over a gentle heat and sauté the onion for about 7 minutes until translucent. Add the garlic and chilies and sauté for an additional minute. Transfer to a bowl and allow to cool. Add the cilantro and season to taste with salt and pepper. **THREE** Divide the cilantro mixture into quarters and use each quarter to stuff a trout, rubbing some of the mixture inside the slashes in the sides of the fish. **FOUR** Cut 4 x 12 inch squares of waxed paper. Brush one side of each paper square with a little oil, leaving the edges free. Place each trout on one half of the oiled side of a paper square. Fold the paper over the fish and twist the side edges together, pressing hard to seal and form a parcel (papillotte). **FIVE** Place the papillottes on a lightly oiled baking sheet and bake in a preheated oven, 400°F, for 18–20 minutes until the fish is cooked. **SIX** Serve immediately, allowing each diner to open their own papillotte at the table.

Serves 4

NUTRIENT ANALYSIS PER SERVING 1155 kJ – 275 cal – 37 g protein – 1 g carbohydrate – 1 g sugars – 14 g fat – 3 g saturated fat – 0 g fiber – 96 mg sodium

HEALTHY TIP Trout, which is high in omega-3 polyunsaturated fatty acids, can cut the risk of heart attacks by lowering blood fat levels and reducing blood clotting. It is an excellent source of vitamins and minerals, and also contains natural oils that help to keep the skin and hair in good condition. It is recommended to eat at least one portion of oily fish a week.

Jumbo shrimp brochettes with ajillo oil

Shrimp are a favorite shellfish of Mexicans. They abound in the Gulf of Mexico as well as on the Pacific Coast, and are used to prepare many regional dishes. This combination of garlic and *guajillo* chili, fried in olive oil—*ajillo*—is traditionally served in restaurants in the central regions of the country.

INGREDIENTS *20 uncooked large jumbo shrimp, in their shells (with heads intact)*

MARINADE *¼ onion, chopped ‖ 1–2 garlic cloves, chopped ‖ 2 tablespoons olive oil ‖ salt and freshly ground black pepper*

AJILLO OIL *2 guajillo chilies ‖ 4 tablespoons olive oil ‖ 5 garlic cloves, peeled but kept whole*

ONE Peel the shrimp, keeping the heads and tails on (for presentation purposes). Make a small cut down the center of the back of each shrimp and carefully remove the black vein. Rinse and pat dry. **TWO** Puree the marinade ingredients in a blender or food processor. Spread the marinade over the shrimp, cover, and allow to marinate in the refrigerator for at least 30 minutes. **THREE** To make the ajillo oil, cut the chilies into thin rings, discarding the seeds. Heat the oil in a small saucepan over a medium heat and gently sauté the garlic cloves until golden brown. Add the chili rings and quickly sauté for a few seconds, then remove from the heat, stir, and allow to infuse for at least 15 minutes. Transfer to a serving bowl and keep at room temperature. **FOUR** Preheat the broiler to medium-high. Thread the shrimp onto metal skewers and cook the brochettes under the broiler for 2–3 minutes, turning halfway through, until the shrimp are cooked—they are ready when they have turned pink and curled up. **FIVE** Place the brochettes on a warm serving plate, sprinkle with the *ajillo* oil and serve immediately.

Serves 4

NUTRIENT ANALYSIS PER SERVING 805 kJ – 195 cal – 9 g protein – 1 g carbohydrate – 1 g sugars – 17 g fat – 2 g saturated fat – 0 g fiber – 96 mg sodium

HEALTHY TIP Shrimp are naturally low in saturated fat. They are an excellent source of protein and also contain a number of essential nutrients, such as magnesium, which plays a role in bone development and nerve and muscle function, zinc, which is good for growth, and selenium, an important antioxidant. Garlic is well known for its antibacterial, antioxidant, and antiseptic properties.

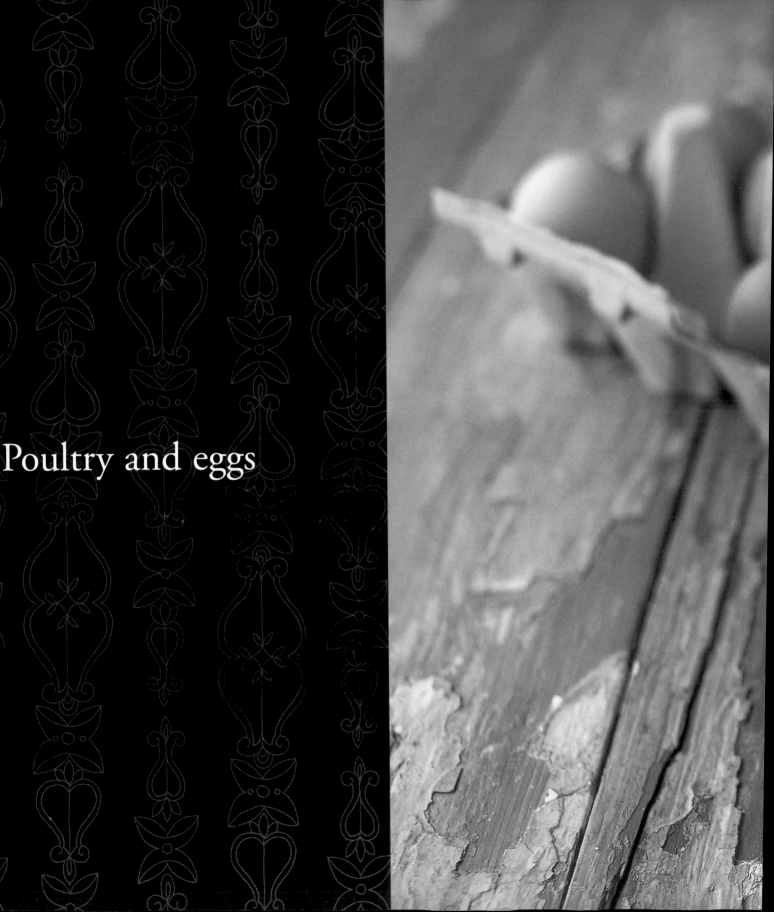

Poultry and eggs

Huevos rancheros

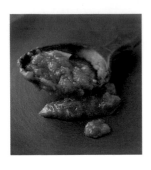

In this internationally famed dish, fried eggs are placed over a corn tortilla, then covered with a delicious tomato sauce. This is a classic item of the Mexican breakfast menu and is traditionally served with black beans and extra tortillas or crusty white bread to mop up every bit of the delicious sauce.

INGREDIENTS *4 soft corn tortillas* ‖ *vegetable oil, for brushing* ‖ *8 large organic free-range eggs*

RANCHERA SAUCE *4 medium-large ripe tomatoes* ‖ *½ onion, roughly chopped* ‖ *1 garlic clove, roughly chopped* ‖ *4 green chilies, roughly chopped (seeded for a milder taste)* ‖ *1 tablespoon vegetable oil* ‖ *salt* ‖ *chopped flat leaf parsley, to garnish (optional)*

ONE First make the sauce. Put the tomatoes, onion, garlic, and chilies in a blender or food processor and blend to a fairly smooth texture. **TWO** Heat the oil in a medium saucepan over a medium heat, add the tomato mixture and simmer for about 10 minutes, or until cooked, stirring constantly. Add salt to taste and keep warm until required. **THREE** Preheat a large, dry heavy skillet over a medium heat. Brush the tortillas with oil and warm each side of 2–3 tortillas at a time in the hot pan for about 30 seconds until soft. Cover with foil to keep warm. **FOUR** Preheat a dry nonstick skillet over a medium heat. Break the eggs, 2 at a time, into the pan and cook over a low heat until the whites have set. **FIVE** Put one tortilla on each plate and place 2 cooked eggs on top. Spoon the ranchera sauce generously over the whites of the eggs, leaving the yolks exposed, and serve immediately with flat leaf parsley sprinkled over the top, if desired.

Serves 4

NUTRIENT ANALYSIS PER SERVING 1485 kJ – 355 cal – 19 g protein – 26 g carbohydrate – 3 g sugars – 19 g fat – 4 g saturated fat – 2 g fiber – 275 mg sodium

HEALTHY TIP To reduce the amount of oil traditionally used in this dish, in this recipe the eggs are cooked in a dry nonstick skillet, and the tortillas are brushed with a little oil instead of being deep-fried.

Scrambled eggs Mexican-style

These delicious scrambled eggs with chopped tomato, onion, and green chili are known as "a la mexicana" because the colors of these last three ingredients echo the colors of the Mexican flag. This is a typical breakfast dish and combines naturally with warm soft corn tortillas, beans, and any Mexican salsa.

INGREDIENTS *1½ tablespoons vegetable oil* ‖ *½ onion, finely chopped* ‖ *8 large organic free-range eggs, beaten* ‖ *3 plum tomatoes, skinned, seeded, and finely chopped* ‖ *2 green chilies, chopped (seeded for a milder taste)* ‖ *salt*

ONE Heat the oil in a large heavy skillet and gently sauté the onion until soft. **TWO** Pour in the beaten eggs, chopped tomatoes, and chilies. Season with salt. Gently stir the egg mixture over the heat until set to your taste. **THREE** Place on a warm dish and serve immediately.

Serves 4

NUTRIENT ANALYSIS PER SERVING 900 kJ – 217 cal – 15 g protein – 3 g carbohydrate – 3 g sugars – 16 g fat – 4 g saturated fat – 1 g fiber – 164 mg sodium

HEALTHY TIP Scrambling the eggs helps to break down their protein, making them much easier to digest. However, if you are concerned about your cholesterol level, try this recipe using the whites only—they provide more than half of the eggs' protein, potassium, and riboflavin, and contain no cholesterol.

"Divorced" eggs

This specialty dish for breakfast in Mexico City, similar to Huevos Rancheros (see page 74), consists of two fried eggs placed over fried corn tortillas and covered with a red sauce over one egg and green sauce over the other. It is commonly served with black beans.

INGREDIENTS *4 soft corn tortillas* ‖ *vegetable oil, for brushing* ‖ *8 large organic free-range eggs*

RED SAUCE *4 medium-large ripe tomatoes* ‖ *½ onion, roughly chopped* ‖ *1 garlic clove, roughly chopped* ‖ *4 green chilies, roughly chopped* ‖ *1 tablespoon vegetable oil* ‖ *salt*

GREEN SAUCE *8 oz tomatillos, husks removed* ‖ *⅓ cup cilantro* ‖ *¼ onion* ‖ *2 green chilies (seeded for a milder taste)* ‖ *salt*

ONE To make the red sauce, put the tomatoes, onion, garlic, and chilies in a blender or food processor and blend to a fairly smooth texture. Heat the oil in a medium saucepan over a medium heat, add the tomato mixture and cook for about 10 minutes, or until cooked, stirring constantly. Season to taste with salt and keep warm until required. **TWO** Puree all the green sauce ingredients in a blender or food processor. Heat the tomatillo mixture in a medium saucepan over a medium heat, season to taste with salt and keep warm until required. **THREE** Preheat a large, dry heavy skillet over a medium heat. Brush the tortillas with oil and warm each side of 2–3 tortillas at a time in the hot pan for about 30 seconds until soft. Cover with foil to keep warm. **FOUR** Preheat a dry nonstick skillet over a medium heat. Break the eggs, 2 at a time, into the pan and cook over a low heat until the whites have set. **FIVE** Put one tortilla on each plate and place 2 cooked eggs on top. Spoon red sauce generously over the white of one of the eggs, leaving the yolk exposed, then spoon green sauce generously over the white of the other egg. Repeat with the remaining eggs. Serve immediately.

Serves 4

NUTRIENT ANALYSIS PER SERVING 1455 kJ – 346 cal – 20 g protein – 30 g carbohydrate – 6 g sugars – 17 g fat – 4 g saturated fat – 4 g fiber – 280 mg sodium

HEALTHY TIP This is a healthy, nutritious dish for breakfast, rich in vitamins, minerals, and high-quality protein from the eggs. The ingredients used for the sauces are also a good source of dietary fiber. Using a dry, nonstick skillet to cook the eggs minimizes the oil content of the dish.

"Rabo de mestiza" poached eggs

This colorful dish is an exciting blend of textures and flavors where the eggs are poached in a tomato sauce with poblano chili strips and garnished with fresh white cheese —sometimes topped with a generous dollop of cream. It is commonly eaten as a main course during Lent.

INGREDIENTS *2 poblano chilies* ‖ *1½ lb ripe tomatoes* ‖ *1 onion, roughly chopped* ‖ *2 garlic cloves, roughly chopped* ‖ *2 cups chicken stock* ‖ *1½ tablespoons vegetable oil* ‖ *1 bay leaf* ‖ *8 large organic free-range eggs* ‖ *2 oz mozzarella cheese, cut into julienne strips* ‖ *salt* ‖ *chopped cilantro leaves, to garnish* ‖ *warm soft corn tortillas, to serve*

ONE Carefully hold the chilies over a high gas flame with metal kitchen tongs or put in a preheated dry heavy skillet over a high heat, turning frequently, until the skins are charred. Put the roasted chilies in a plastic bag, wrap the bag with a dish towel, and allow to sweat for at least 15 minutes. Remove the skins, rinse the chilies under cold running water and discard the stems and seeds. Pat dry and slice lengthwise into strips. **TWO** Put the tomatoes, onion, garlic, and half the stock in a blender or food processor and blend to a fairly smooth texture. Pass the mixture through a strainer. **THREE** Heat the oil in a heavy saucepan (10 inches in diameter) over a medium heat, add the tomato mixture and bay leaf and gently simmer for 15–20 minutes until cooked, stirring occasionally. Add the poblano strips and, if the sauce is too thick, add some more of the remaining stock. Bring to a boil and season to taste with salt. **FOUR** Break the eggs, one at a time, into the sauce, cover and cook over a gentle heat for a few minutes until the whites have set. Just before removing from the heat, add the mozzarella. **FIVE** Serve immediately, garnished with cilantro and accompanied by warm corn tortillas.

Serves 4

NUTRIENT ANALYSIS PER SERVING 1187 kJ – 284 cal – 19 g protein – 8 g carbohydrate – 7 g sugars – 20 g fat – 6 g saturated fat – 3 g fiber – 456 mg sodium

HEALTHY TIP Eggs are a good source of high-quality protein, low in fat and rich in vitamin A, and also contain many of the B group vitamins and minerals. In addition, tomatoes are an excellent source of antioxidants, including vitamins A and C, and they also contain potassium and dietary fiber.

Green bean omelet with pasilla chili sauce

This is a favorite way of enjoying eggs and fresh green beans. The pasilla chili sauce adds an elegant touch to the omelet. It makes a tasty and nutritious lunch, served with a healthy salad and crusty bread.

INGREDIENTS *½ cup green beans ‖ 8 large organic free-range eggs ‖ 4 teaspoons unsalted butter ‖ salt and freshly ground black pepper ‖ flat leaf parsley, to garnish ‖ warm tortillas, to serve*

PASILLA CHILI SAUCE *4 pasilla chilies ‖ ¼ onion ‖ 1 garlic clove, unpeeled ‖ 1 teaspoon vegetable oil ‖ salt*

ONE First make the sauce. Remove the stems from the chilies, tear the chilies open and remove the seeds (for a milder sauce, remove all the stringy, light-colored veins as well). Heat a dry heavy skillet over a medium heat and lightly roast for a few seconds on both sides. Transfer to a heatproof bowl, cover with boiling water, and allow to soak for 15–20 minutes until soft. **TWO** Put the onion and garlic clove on the hot surface of the skillet and cook, turning occasionally, until soft. Allow to cool, then peel the garlic. **THREE** Drain the chilies and transfer to a blender or food processor with some of their soaking water, add the onion and garlic and blend until smooth. Pass the mixture through a strainer. **FOUR** Heat the oil in a heavy saucepan over a medium heat, add the chili mixture, and gently simmer for about 15 minutes until cooked. Season to taste with salt. Keep warm until required. **FIVE** Meanwhile, steam the green beans for 5–10 minutes, depending on thickness, until just tender, cut them into ½ inch pieces and set aside. **SIX** Break 2 eggs into a bowl and beat with a fork until frothy. Season with salt and pepper. Heat 1 teaspoon of the butter in an omelet pan. When sizzling, pour in the eggs and cook over a medium heat, gently stirring, until the bottom has set and the top is still creamy. Sprinkle over a quarter of the green beans, fold in half and transfer to a warm dish. Pour some of the sauce on top. Repeat with the remaining butter, eggs, and beans. **SEVEN** Serve immediately with warm tortillas and flat leaf parsley sprinkled over the top.

Serves 4

NUTRIENT ANALYSIS PER SERVING 955 kJ – 230 cal – 15 g protein – 1 g carbohydrate – 1 g sugars – 18 g fat – 7 g saturated fat – 1 g fiber – 166 mg sodium

HEALTHY TIP If you are concerned with your fat intake, use a nonstick omelet pan and reduce the amount of butter even further. Green beans are low in calories and rich in nutrients such as vitamin C, vitamin K, manganese, and dietary fiber, among others. Steaming them helps to retain their nutrients.

Chicken mixiotes in almond and chili sauce

Mixiote is the tough outer skin of the maguey, a plant belonging to the succulent family. It was traditionally used to wrap bite-size portions of marinated meat with sauce into small parcels, tied with string. Nowadays, it is common to use waxed paper instead of maguey skin to prepare this dish.

INGREDIENTS *4 x 6 oz boneless, skinless chicken breasts, diced* ‖ *warm soft corn tortillas, to serve*

SAUCE *3 ancho chilies* ‖ *1 tomato* ‖ *¼ onion, roughly chopped* ‖ *2 garlic cloves, unpeeled* ‖ *¾ cup chicken stock* ‖ *1 tablespoon vegetable oil* ‖ *⅓ cup almonds with skins on, ground* ‖ *¼ teaspoon dried oregano* ‖ *pinch of dried thyme* ‖ *salt*

ONE First make the sauce. Remove the stems from the chilies, tear the chilies open and remove the seeds (for a milder sauce, remove all the stringy, light-colored veins as well). Heat a dry heavy skillet over a medium heat and lightly roast the chilies for a few seconds on both sides. Transfer to a heatproof bowl, cover with boiling water, and allow to soak for 15–20 minutes until soft. **TWO** Meanwhile, put the tomato, onion, and garlic cloves on the hot surface of the skillet and roast, turning occasionally, until soft. Allow to cool, then peel the garlic. **THREE** Drain the chilies and transfer to a blender or food processor. Add the tomato, onion, garlic, and the stock and blend until smooth. Pass the mixture through a strainer. **FOUR** Heat the oil in a heavy saucepan, add the chili mixture, almonds, and herbs and simmer for about 15 minutes, stirring constantly, until the sauce is cooked. Season to taste with salt and allow to cool completely. **FIVE** Put the chicken in a glass bowl, add the sauce and mix together well. Cover and allow to marinate in the refrigerator for at least 2 hours. **SIX** Cut 4 x 9½ inch squares of waxed paper. Place a quarter of the chicken mixture in the center of each square, pull up the sides and make 4 parcels. Tie securely with string. **SEVEN** Place the parcels in an ovenproof dish inside a large roasting pan half-filled with hot water, making sure that the water does not touch the parcels. Steam-bake in a preheated oven, 350°F, for 50 minutes until the chicken is cooked through and tender. **EIGHT** Serve hot, letting each diner untie their own mixiote, with warm corn tortillas.

Serves 4

NUTRIENT ANALYSIS PER SERVING 1330 kJ – 317 cal – 42 g protein – 3 g carbohydrate – 2 g sugars – 16 g fat – 3 g saturated fat – 2 g fiber – 335 mg sodium

HEALTHY TIP Steaming is the healthiest cooking method, as fewer nutrients are lost or destroyed. Flavors and textures also remain more intact than with frying or boiling in water.

Turkey with Xico-style mole sauce

This mole (from the Nahuatl word *Molli*, meaning sauce) is from Xico in the state of Veracruz. Prepare the mole paste in advance and let the flavor develop.

INGREDIENTS *1 x 4–6½ lb whole turkey breast, halved ‖ 1 onion ‖ 4 garlic cloves, peeled but kept whole ‖ plain White Rice (see page 41—omit the Poblano Chili Strips), to serve ‖ chopped flat leaf parsley, to garnish (optional)*

MOLE SAUCE *4 oz mulato chilies ‖ 1½ oz pasilla chilies ‖ ¾ oz ancho chilies ‖ ½ large onion, chopped ‖ 3 garlic cloves, peeled but kept whole ‖ 10 oz tomatoes ‖ 5 tablespoons vegetable oil ‖ 2 soft corn tortillas ‖ 1 petit pain ‖ ⅓ cup pitted prunes ‖ 3 tablespoons raisins ‖ ¼ plantain ‖ 2½ tablespoons blanched almonds, toasted ‖ ¼ cup blanched hazelnuts, toasted ‖ 3 tablespoons pine nuts, toasted ‖ 3 tablespoons sesame seeds, toasted, plus 1 tablespoon to garnish ‖ ¼ cup walnuts, toasted ‖ ¼ teaspoon aniseed ‖ ½ cinnamon stick, broken and toasted ‖ 2 whole cloves, toasted ‖ 3 allspice berries, toasted ‖ 5 black peppercorns, toasted ‖ ¼ cup brown sugar ‖ salt*

ONE Put the turkey, onion, and garlic cloves in a saucepan, cover with water, and bring to a boil. Simmer for 1–1½ hours until cooked, skimming off any scum. Lift out the turkey, strain the broth and allow to cool. Refrigerate until required. **TWO** Remove the stems from the chilies, tear the chilies open and remove the seeds, then roast for a few seconds on both sides in a hot skillet. Soak them in boiling water for 20 minutes until soft. **THREE** Roast the onion, garlic cloves and tomatoes in the skillet until soft. **FOUR** Transfer the chilies with some of their soaking water, onion, garlic, and tomatoes to a blender or food processor and blend to a smooth texture, then sieve. **FIVE** Heat half of the oil in a saucepan, pour in the chili mixture and simmer for about 20 minutes, stirring occasionally. **SIX** Heat the remaining oil in a skillet and, one at a time, briefly sauté the tortillas, bread, prunes, raisins, and plantain. Blend these with some of the chili mixture to a smooth texture. Add to the remaining chili mixture. **SEVEN** Grind the nuts, seeds, and spices, add to the sauce and simmer for about 45 minutes, stirring constantly until it is a thick paste. Add some turkey broth to adjust the consistency. Add the sugar and salt to taste. **EIGHT** Slice the turkey, add to the sauce and simmer for 10 minutes. Serve the turkey with the sauce spooned over and garnished with sesame seeds and flat leaf parsley, if desired, with the White Rice.

Serves 8

NUTRIENT ANALYSIS PER SERVING 2216 kJ – 530 cal – 44 g protein – 27 g carbohydrate – 15 g sugars – 28 g fat – 5 g saturated fat – 4 g fiber – 204 mg sodium

HEALTHY TIP The turkey is a good source of proteins and some B vitamins.

Duck tacos

Duck was eaten in Mexico before the arrival of the Spanish. It is mainly consumed in the southern states of the country. Duck tacos are a traditional dish, typically served with a very hot sauce in Mexico City bars where workers go to drink, eat, and even play a few rounds of dominoes.

INGREDIENTS *1 x 3½ lb hot roasted duck* ‖ *16 soft corn tortillas* ‖ *1 onion, finely chopped* ‖ *8 green chilies, chopped (seeded for a milder taste)* ‖ *⅓ cup cilantro, finely chopped* ‖ *salt* ‖ *finely chopped tomato, to garnish (optional)* ‖ *salsa of your choice, to serve*

ONE Shred the duck meat, discard any fat and keep warm. **TWO** Preheat a large, dry heavy skillet over a medium heat. Warm each side of the tortillas, 2–3 at a time, for about 30 seconds in the hot pan until soft. Transfer to a basket and cover with a clean dish towel. **THREE** Put a portion of shredded duck on top of one warm tortilla, sprinkle some of the onion, chilies, and cilantro on top, add salt to taste, roll up and place on a warm platter. Cover with the clean dish towel. Repeat with the remaining ingredients. **FOUR** Serve immediately with your favorite salsa and garnish with the chopped tomato, if desired.

Serves 4

NUTRIENT ANALYSIS PER SERVING (using 16 x 1½ oz tortillas 3430 kJ – 816 cal – 54 g protein – 93 g carbohydrate – 2 g sugars – 25 g fat – 4 g saturated fat – 5 g fiber – 570 mg sodium

HEALTHY TIP Duck can be high in fat, so always remove the skin and as much fat as possible to make this nutritious dish healthier.

Meat

Beef brochettes with salsa mexicana

The colors of the ingredients of salsa mexicana are those of the Mexican flag: green, white, and red, from the chilies and cilantro, onions, and tomatoes. Its vibrant flavor matches its visual impact, and makes a healthful accompaniment to these succulent brochettes.

INGREDIENTS *1 lb beef tenderloin* ‖ *1 red onion* ‖ *2 green bell peppers* ‖ *olive oil, for brushing* ‖ *salt and freshly ground black pepper*

SALSA MEXICANA *4 large ripe tomatoes, skinned, seeded, and finely chopped* ‖ *½ onion, finely chopped* ‖ *3 green chilies, finely chopped* ‖ *2 tablespoons finely chopped cilantro* ‖ *1 teaspoon freshly squeezed lime juice (optional)* ‖ *1 tablespoon extra virgin olive oil (optional)* ‖ *salt*

ONE Soak 4 bamboo skewers in cold water for 30 minutes. To make the salsa, mix together the tomatoes, onion, chilies, and cilantro, add the lime juice and oil, if using, and season to taste with salt. Transfer to a serving bowl and keep at room temperature. **TWO** Cut the beef into 16 bite-size cubes. Cut the red onion and bell peppers into 1 inch squares. Thread the beef cubes onto the bamboo skewers, alternating with the onion and green peppers. Brush the brochettes with oil and season with salt and pepper just before cooking. **THREE** Cook the brochettes under a preheated high broiler for 4–5 minutes, turning halfway, until the meat is cooked according to your taste. **FOUR** Serve the brochettes with the salsa mexicana on the side.

Serves 4

NUTRIENT ANALYSIS PER SERVING 924 kJ – 219 cal – 28 g protein – 10 g carbohydrate – 9 g sugars – 8 g fat – 3 g saturated fat – 4 g fiber – 95 mg sodium

HEALTHY TIP Tomatoes are rich in vitamin C and also contain vitamins A and B, potassium, iron, and phosphorus. A medium tomato has almost as much fiber as a slice of whole-wheat bread and only about 35 calories.

Meatballs in chipotle sauce

This dish of spicy meatballs—*albondigas*—cooked in a tomato and chipotle chili sauce is a well-loved one in the central regions of the country and is served at lunchtime at home as well as in restaurants and bars. It is a very popular take-out dish in many markets.

INGREDIENTS *8 oz lean ground pork* ‖ *8 oz lean ground beef* ‖ *½ small onion, finely chopped* ‖ *1 garlic clove, crushed* ‖ *1 organic free-range egg* ‖ *salt and freshly ground black pepper*

CHIPOTLE SAUCE *3 chipotle chilies* ‖ *2 lb tomatoes* ‖ *½ small onion* ‖ *1 garlic clove, peeled but kept whole* ‖ *1 tablespoon vegetable oil* ‖ *1 bay leaf* ‖ *1 thyme sprig* ‖ *salt*

TO SERVE *plain White Rice (see page 41—omit the Poblano Chili Strips)* ‖ *warm soft corn tortillas* ‖ *chopped flat leaf parsley (optional)*

ONE First make the sauce. Remove the stems from the chilies, tear the chilies open and remove the seeds (for a milder sauce, remove all the stringy, light-colored veins as well). Heat a dry heavy skillet over a medium heat and lightly roast the chilies for a few seconds on both sides. Transfer to a heatproof bowl, cover with boiling water, and allow to soak for 15–20 minutes until soft. **TWO** Meanwhile, put the tomatoes, onion, and garlic clove on the hot surface of the skillet and roast, turning occasionally, until soft. **THREE** Drain the chilies and transfer to a blender or food processor. Add the tomatoes, onion, and garlic and blend to a fairly smooth texture, adding a little of the chili soaking water if necessary. Pass through a strainer. **FOUR** Heat the oil in a heavy saucepan over a medium heat, add the sauce and gently simmer with the bay leaf and thyme sprig for about 15 minutes until cooked. Season to taste with salt. **FIVE** Meanwhile, to make the meatballs, mix the ground meats, onion, garlic, egg, and salt and pepper together in a bowl—for the best result, wear rubber gloves and use your hands. Shape the mixture into chestnut-size balls. When the sauce is cooked, add the meatballs and bring to a boil. Reduce the heat, cover and gently simmer for about 35 minutes until cooked through and tender. **SIX** Serve immediately with the plain White Rice (see page 41) and warm corn tortillas, with the parsley sprinkled over the top, if desired.

Serves 4

NUTRIENT ANALYSIS PER SERVING 1115 kJ – 266 cal – 30 g protein – 9 g carbohydrate – 9 g sugars – 12 g fat – 4 g saturated fat – 4 g fiber – 129 mg sodium

HEALTHY TIP Besides being delicious, meat has a very high nutritional value. Choose the leanest cuts of meat and ask your butcher to grind them.

Pork tenderloin in pumpkin seed sauce

Pumpkin seed sauce, known as *pipián*, is a pre-Hispanic sauce, and used to be served with fish or game before the arrival of the Spanish, who introduced pork to the country. This delicious and delicate sauce is prepared with *pepitas*—pumpkin seeds—which are a highly nutritious and a very popular ingredient in Mexican cooking.

INGREDIENTS *1½ lb pork tenderloin ‖ salt ‖ plain White Rice (see page 41—omit the Poblano Chili Strips), to serve*

PUMPKIN SEED SAUCE *1 lb tomatillos, husks removed ‖ 5 green chilies ‖ 2 garlic cloves, unpeeled ‖ ¼ cup cilantro ‖ 4 cups chicken stock ‖ 2 tablespoons vegetable oil ‖ 2 ½ cups pumpkin seeds, shelled and toasted, plus extra to garnish ‖ salt*

ONE Lightly sprinkle the pork tenderloin with salt. Place in a roasting pan and roast in a preheated oven, 425°F, for 20 minutes. Reduce the oven temperature to 350°F, and roast for an additional 30 minutes or until thoroughly cooked. **TWO** Meanwhile, to make the sauce, heat a dry heavy skillet over a medium heat and roast the tomatillos, chilies, and garlic cloves, turning occasionally, until soft. Allow to cool, then peel the garlic. **THREE** Transfer the tomatillos, chilies, and garlic to a blender or food processor, add the cilantro and half the stock and blend to a fairly smooth texture. Pass through a strainer. **FOUR** Heat the oil in a heavy saucepan over a medium heat and gently simmer the sauce for about 10 minutes until cooked. Season to taste with salt. **FIVE** Transfer the mixture again to a blender or food processor, add the pumpkin seeds and the remaining stock and blend to a fairly smooth texture. Check the seasoning. Place in a heatproof dish and keep warm in a large saucepan half-filled with water over a low heat. **SIX** When the meat is ready, transfer the tenderloin to a warm serving dish, cover loosely with foil and allow to rest for 10 minutes before carving. Slice the pork and serve with the pumpkin seed sauce and the plain White Rice (see page 41), sprinkled with pumpkin seeds to garnish.

Serves 4

NUTRIENT ANALYSIS PER SERVING 2944 kJ – 707 cal – 56 g protein – 13 g carbohydrate – 4 g sugars – 48 g fat – 10 g saturated fat – 1 g fiber – 370 mg sodium

HEALTHY TIP Pork tenderloin is an excellent source of protein and thiamine (vitamin B1), essential for energy production, nerve function, and muscle tone. The pumpkin seeds are a very good source of several nutrients including manganese, magnesium, and phosphorus, as well as protein and monounsaturated fats.

Leg of lamb with adobo sauce

Adobo is a sauce made from pureed dried chilies, herbs, and vinegar as the main ingredients. It is used as a serving sauce as well as a marinade for meats. This aromatic sauce complements the flavor of the lamb perfectly in this recipe.

INGREDIENTS *1 x 3–4 lb leg of lamb ‖ 1 tablespoon olive oil ‖ 2 garlic cloves, crushed ‖ salt and freshly ground black pepper ‖ wild arugula leaves, to garnish (optional)*
ADOBO SAUCE *4–5 ancho chilies, seeded ‖ 1 small onion ‖ 4 garlic cloves ‖ 1 teaspoon dried oregano ‖ ½ teaspoon dried thyme ‖ 2 tablespoons cider vinegar ‖ 1¼ cups chicken stock ‖ 1 tablespoon vegetable oil*

ONE Rub the lamb with the oil and garlic, season with salt and pepper and place in a roasting pan. Roast in a preheated oven, 425°F, for 20 minutes. Reduce the oven temperature to 350°F, and roast for an additional 25 minutes per lb, basting occasionally. The meat should still be pink inside. **TWO** Meanwhile, to make the sauce, remove the stems from the chilies, tear the chilies open and remove the seeds. Heat a dry, heavy skillet over a medium heat and lightly roast the chilies for a few seconds on both sides. Transfer to a heatproof bowl, cover with boiling water and allow to soak for 15–20 minutes until soft. **THREE** Drain the chilies and transfer to a blender or food processor. Add the remaining ingredients, except the oil, and process until smooth. Pass through a strainer. **FOUR** Heat the oil in a saucepan over a medium heat, add the chili mixture and simmer gently, stirring constantly, for about 15 minutes until cooked. If the sauce gets too thick, add a little more stock. Keep warm. **FIVE** When the meat is ready, transfer to a warm plate and cover loosely with foil. Allow to rest for 10 minutes before carving. Slice the meat and serve covered with the adobo sauce, garnished with arugula leaves if desired.

Serves 4

NUTRIENT ANALYSIS PER SERVING 1485 kJ – 360 cal – 57 g protein – 3 g carbohydrate – 2 g sugars – 34 g fat – 13 g saturated fat – 0 g fiber – 1344 mg sodium

HEALTHY TIP Lamb is a good source of protein and essential vitamins and minerals, such as zinc, which is highly valuable for its beneficial effects on the immune system.

Beef salpicón

A *salpicón* is a combination of different ingredients including shredded meat or fish. In the Yucatan Peninsula, in the south of the country, it is prepared in the old-fashioned way using shredded venison. Since deer is a protected species, beef is now more commonly used to prepare this traditional dish.

INGREDIENTS *1 lb stewing beef, cut into large squares* ‖ *½ onion, kept whole, and ½ onion, finely chopped* ‖ *1 garlic clove, peeled* ‖ *1 celery stick* ‖ *1 bay leaf* ‖ *2 tablespoons finely chopped cilantro* ‖ *6–8 romaine lettuce leaves, finely shredded* ‖ *1 large ripe avocado, peeled, pitted, and diced* ‖ *1 large tomato, diced* ‖ *2 chipotle chilies, bottled or canned in adobo sauce, seeded and finely sliced, or 2–3 green chilies, seeded and cut into thin strips* ‖ *6 radishes, finely sliced* ‖ *3 oz feta cheese, crumbled* ‖ *salt and freshly ground black pepper*

DRESSING *⅔ cup extra virgin olive oil* ‖ *3 tablespoons cider vinegar* ‖ *½ teaspoon dried oregano* ‖ *salt and freshly ground black pepper*

ONE Put the meat in a saucepan and cover with water. Bring to a boil, skimming the scum that rises to the surface. Add the whole onion half, garlic clove, celery, bay leaf, salt and pepper to taste. Cover and simmer for 1½–2 hours until the meat is very tender. Allow to cool slightly in the broth. **TWO** Remove the meat from the broth and shred into fine strands (reserve the broth for some other use). Add the chopped onion and cilantro. Mix all the dressing ingredients together and pour two thirds over the meat. Mix well, cover, and allow to stand for 20 minutes. **THREE** Just before serving, make a bed of shredded lettuce in a serving dish. Place the meat mixture on the lettuce. Garnish with pieces of avocado alternating with the tomato and chipotle slices or green chili strips. Drizzle the remaining dressing over the salad. Sprinkle with the radish slices and the feta, and serve immediately.

Serves 4

NUTRIENT ANALYSIS PER SERVING 3060 kJ – 740 cal – 30 g protein – 4 g carbohydrate – 3 g sugars – 67 g fat – 19 g saturated fat – 1 g fiber – 350 mg sodium

HEALTHY TIP Combining the meat with vegetables provides both high-quality protein from the meat and dietary fiber and other nutrients from the vegetables.

Beef and vegetable casserole with dried chili sauce

This is one of the most delicious and healthy stews in Mexican cuisine. Meat and vegetables are gently cooked and seasoned with dried chilies. Traditionally, small balls made with masa harina—*chochoyotes*—are cooked in the broth.

INGREDIENTS *1¼ lb stewing beef or top round, diced* ‖ *1 onion* ‖ *2 garlic cloves, 1 peeled* ‖ *1 celery stick* ‖ *1 bay leaf* ‖ *5 black peppercorns* ‖ *2 corn ears, cut into chunks* ‖ *2 zucchini, halved and cut lengthwise into quarters* ‖ *1 carrot, halved and cut lengthwise into quarters* ‖ *5 pasilla chilies* ‖ *1 teaspoon vegetable oil* ‖ *2 fresh epazote sprigs (if available)* ‖ *½ cup masa harina* ‖ *salt* ‖ *warm soft corn tortillas, to serve*

ONE Put the meat in a saucepan and cover with water. Bring to a boil, skimming the scum that rises to the surface. Add half the onion, the peeled garlic clove, celery, bay leaf, and peppercorns. Cover and simmer for 1½–2 hours until the meat is tender. Remove the meat from the broth, strain the broth, and reserve. **TWO** Cook the corn, zucchini, and carrot separately in boiling water until just tender. Strain and reserve the vegetables and cooking water. **THREE** Remove the stems from the chilies, tear the chilies open and remove the seeds. Heat a dry heavy skillet over a medium heat and lightly roast the chilies for a few seconds on both sides. Soak the chilies in boiling water for 15–20 minutes until soft. **FOUR** Meanwhile, place the unpeeled garlic and the remaining onion, halved, in the skillet and roast, turning occasionally, until soft. Allow to cool, then peel the garlic. **FIVE** Drain the chilies and transfer to a blender or food processor with some of the soaking water. Add the garlic and onion and blend until smooth, then sieve. **SIX** Heat the oil in a saucepan, add the chili mixture and simmer for about 15 minutes. Add the meat broth, epazote, and salt to taste. **SEVEN** Mix the masa harina with about 5 tablespoons water and knead to a soft dough. Mold into ½ inch balls and press your finger into the center of each. Add to the casserole and gently simmer for 15 minutes. **EIGHT** Add the meat and vegetables, with some of the reserved vegetable cooking water, if needed. Check the seasoning and simmer for an additional 10 minutes. Serve very hot in warmed individual soup plates with warm corn tortillas.

Serves 4

NUTRIENT ANALYSIS PER SERVING 1687 kJ – 403 cal – 35 g protein – 22 g carbohydrate – 4 g sugars – 20 g fat – 7 g saturated fat – 2 g fiber – 323 mg sodium

HEALTHY TIP Beef is an excellent source of protein, potassium, zinc, and certain B complex vitamins. The vegetables are low in fat, contain no cholesterol and provide soluble and insoluble fiber.

Vegetables and salads

Watercress, grapefruit, and avocado salad

Watercress is extensively cultivated in the center of the country and is usually eaten raw in salads, as in this colorful dish, whose ingredients offer an elegant combination of flavors and textures.

INGREDIENTS *2 red or pink grapefruit* ‖ *2 large ripe avocados* ‖ *1 cup watercress, washed* ‖ *8–10 small radishes, finely sliced* ‖ *4 green onions, cut diagonally into thin slices*

VINAIGRETTE *6 tablespoons olive oil* ‖ *2 tablespoons cider vinegar* ‖ *½ teaspoon honey* ‖ *½ teaspoon Dijon mustard* ‖ *salt and freshly ground black pepper*

ONE Peel the grapefruit. Divide into segments and remove the membranes and seeds. **TWO** Mix all the vinaigrette ingredients together thoroughly. **THREE** Just before serving, half the avocados and remove the pits. Peel and slice the flesh. Place in a bowl with the remaining salad ingredients. Add the dressing and toss gently. Check the seasoning. **FOUR** Serve in individual salad dishes.

Serves 4

NUTRIENT ANALYSIS PER SERVING 1233 kJ – 297 cal – 3 g protein – 13 g carbohydrate – 12 g sugars – 27 g fat – 4 g saturated fat – 3 g fiber – 40 mg sodium

HEALTHY TIP Watercress is a powerful detoxifier, rich in vitamins and minerals, especially vitamins A and C, zinc, and iron. Grapefruit is an excellent source of vitamin C, which helps to support the immune system. The avocados are a good source of potassium and dietary fiber. They also help toward maintaining a healthy blood pressure.

Green bean and new potato salad

Cooked fresh vegetables are frequently prepared as side dishes throughout the country. This colorful and healthy salad is usually served to accompany fish, meat, or poultry dishes, especially during summertime.

INGREDIENTS *2 cups green beans ‖ 8 oz baby new potatoes, cooked in their skins ‖ ½ red onion, finely sliced, lengthwise ‖ ½ teaspoon dried oregano*

DRESSING *1 tablespoon cider vinegar ‖ 3 tablespoons extra virgin olive oil ‖ 1 small garlic clove, finely chopped ‖ ¼ teaspoon superfine sugar ‖ salt and freshly ground black pepper*

ONE Trim the tops of the green beans, leaving the tails on. Blanch the beans in a saucepan of boiling salted water for 1 minute. Drain and place on a tray to cool rapidly. **TWO** Slice the cooked potatoes diagonally and place them in a large salad bowl. Mix in the red onion and green beans. **THREE** Mix all the dressing ingredients together throroughly, drizzle over the vegetables and toss gently. Arrange the salad on a platter, sprinkle with the oregano and serve immediately.

Serves 4

NUTRIENT ANALYSIS PER SERVING 549 kJ – 132 cal – 2 g protein – 12 g carbohydrate – 4 g sugars – 9 g fat – 1 g saturated fat – 2 g fiber – 7 mg sodium

HEALTHY TIP While relatively low in calories, this salad is loaded with nutrients. Both green beans and potatoes are very good sources of vitamin C, manganese, potassium, calcium, and dietary fiber.

Grilled zucchini with goat cheese

Zucchini are a favorite vegetable in Mexico and are used in many regional dishes. A popular choice is the combination of zucchini with fresh white cheese.

INGREDIENTS *5 large zucchini, diagonally sliced* ‖ *1 tablespoon olive oil* ‖ *salt and freshly ground black pepper* ‖ *1 tablespoon extra virgin olive oil* ‖ *1–2 garlic cloves, finely diced* ‖ *4 oz soft goat cheese* ‖ *3 tablespoons pine nuts, toasted*

ONE Brush the zucchini slices with olive oil and cook in a hot griddle pan for 1–2 minutes each side. The zucchini should be cooked, but still firm. Season to taste with salt and pepper. Heat the extra virgin olive oil in a small skillet over a medium heat and gently sauté the garlic for 1 minute. **TWO** Transfer the zucchini to a warm serving plate. Crumble the goat cheese over the zucchini, sprinkle with the pine nuts and drizzle the garlic oil on top. Serve immediately.

Serves 4

NUTRIENT ANALYSIS PER SERVING 710 kJ – 170 cal – 6 g protein – 3 g carbohydrate – 3 g sugars – 15 g fat – 4 g saturated fat – 1 g fiber – 125 mg sodium

HEALTHY TIP Zucchini are low in calories and a good source of beta-carotene, which the body converts into vitamin A. They also are a useful source of vitamin C and folate. Pine nuts, being high in protein and essential fat, are a good meat substitute for vegetarians.

Pickled vegetables

Pickles are a classic feature of Mexican cuisine. Pickled chilies, especially the jalapeño variety, are a favorite and are usually combined with carrots and onions. Nowadays, a wider selection of pickled vegetables are offered as an appetizer or side dish. Along the coast of Mexico, fish and shellfish pickled dishes are very popular.

INGREDIENTS *3 tablespoons olive oil* ‖ *16 green onions, white parts only* ‖ *4 carrots, cut into sticks* ‖ *4 garlic cloves, peeled* ‖ *2 green chilies, preferably jalapeño* ‖ *½ cup cauliflower florets* ‖ *16 small yellow- or red-skinned potatoes, cooked in their skins* ‖ *5 oz button mushrooms* ‖ *1 ½ cups cider vinegar* ‖ *¾ cup water* ‖ *½ teaspoon dried thyme* ‖ *½ teaspoon dried oregano* ‖ *2 bay leaves* ‖ *1 teaspoon salt* ‖ *freshly ground black pepper*

ONE Heat the oil in a large heavy skillet and sauté the green onions, carrots, and garlic cloves over a medium heat for 2 minutes. Add the chilies (halve to obtain a strong chili flavor) and cauliflower and sauté for 2 minutes. Add the potatoes and mushrooms and sauté for an additional minute. **TWO** Put the vinegar, measured water, herbs, salt and pepper to taste in a saucepan and bring to a boil. Pour over the vegetables, then immediately remove from the heat. Allow to cool completely. **THREE** Pour into a glass container, cover, and refrigerate for at least 1 day before using. **FOUR** To keep long-term, pack into sterilized jars, seal, and store in a cool, dark place for up to 1 year.

Serves 4

NUTRIENT ANALYSIS PER SERVING 880 kJ – 210 cal – 6 g protein – 27 g carbohydrate – 11 g sugars – 10 g fat – 2 g saturated fat – 5 g fiber – 545 mg sodium

HEALTHY TIP In general, vegetables provide a range of vitamins and minerals, particularly A, B6, C, and folic acid. They also provide potassium, iron, magnesium, and calcium, and are low in fat and contain no cholesterol. Choose the best quality fresh vegetables, organic if possible.

Potato patties

Potato patties are prepared all over the country. In central Mexico, especially during Lent, this could be the main dish of a family meal at lunchtime and is traditionally served with lettuce and salsa mexicana.

INGREDIENTS *1 lb potatoes, unpeeled* ‖ *4 oz feta cheese, crumbled* ‖ *1 ½ tablespoons unsalted butter* ‖ *1 organic free-range egg yolk* ‖ *all-purpose flour, for flouring* ‖ *vegetable oil, for oiling* ‖ *salt and freshly ground black pepper*

TO SERVE *lettuce leaves, torn into bite-size pieces (optional)* ‖ *lemon wedges (optional)* ‖ *Salsa Mexicana (see page 90)*

ONE Cook the potatoes whole in their skins in boiling water until tender. Drain and allow to cool slightly. When cool enough to handle, peel, then mash the potatoes while still warm. **TWO** Place the mashed potatoes in a bowl, add the feta, butter, and egg yolk and stir until well mixed. Season to taste with salt and pepper. **THREE** Divide the mixture into 9 equal portions and, with floured hands, shape into flattish circles about 3 inches in diameter. Place on a lightly oiled baking sheet and bake in a preheated oven, 350°F, for about 15 minutes, then turn over and bake for an additional 10 minutes until golden brown. **FOUR** Serve warm with lettuce and lemon wedges, if using, and Salsa Mexicana (see page 90).

Serves 3–4

NUTRIENT ANALYSIS PER SERVING 1394 kJ – 334 cal – 10 g protein – 34 g carbohydrate – 2 g sugars – 18 g fat – 9 g saturated fat – 3 g fiber – 500 mg sodium

HEALTHY TIP Baking the potato cakes in the oven rather than frying them, the traditional cooking method, makes these patties even healthier. Potatoes are very good source of vegetable protein, potassium, vitamin C, iron, phosphorus, niacin, enzymes, and dietary fiber.

Rice pudding

In this popular Spanish dessert, rice is cooked in milk with sugar, cinnamon, and raisins. Its consistency can be liquid or thick and it can be served warm, cold, or at room temperature. In Mexico City it is usually served cold as a lunchtime dessert at home or in restaurants or cafés, while in other parts of the country it is served warm for breakfast.

INGREDIENTS *1 cup long-grain white rice* ‖ *6 cups lowfat milk* ‖ *½ cup superfine sugar* ‖ *pinch of salt* ‖ *1 vanilla bean* ‖ *1 cinnamon stick, broken into 2–3 pieces* ‖ *thinly pared zest of 1 lime* ‖ *thinly pared zest of 1 orange* ‖ *⅓ cup raisins* ‖ *ground cinnamon, to decorate*

ONE Rinse the rice briefly to remove any impurities, drain, and soak for 15 minutes in boiling water. Rinse well and drain. Put the milk, sugar, salt, vanilla bean, cinnamon stick, and lime and orange zest in a heavy saucepan. Bring slowly to the boil, stirring constantly. Remove from the heat and allow to infuse for 10 minutes. Remove the lime and orange zest, then remove the vanilla bean, slit open and scrape out the seeds into the milk. **TWO** Add the rice to the milk and bring to a boil over a medium heat. Reduce the heat, cover, and gently simmer until the rice is cooked and the mixture thickens. Stir in the raisins. You may need some more cold milk to adjust the consistency—the rice must not be dry. **THREE** Remove from the heat and allow to cool, then transfer the pudding to a serving dish, cover, and refrigerate until required. **FOUR** Serve cold, dusted with cinnamon to decorate.

Serves 6–8

NUTRIENT ANALYSIS PER SERVING 1376 kJ – 324 cal – 11 g protein – 65 g carbohydrate – 36 g sugars – 4 g fat – 3 g saturated fat – 1 g fiber – 145 mg sodium

HEALTHY TIP Rice, which is cholesterol- and gluten-free, is low in sodium, contains only a trace of fat and is an excellent source of complex carbohydrates. Lowfat milk is a good source of calcium and contains only 2 percent fat.

Quince paste

Because of its high pectin content, quince is particularly good in jams, jellies, and preserves. Quince paste is of Arab origin and was introduced to Mexico by the Spanish. It is usually served with Manchego cheese or panela, a fresh white Mexican cheese.

INGREDIENTS *2 lb quinces ‖ granulated sugar ‖ 1 cup water ‖ Manchego cheese, to serve*

ONE Wash and quarter the quinces. Place in a saucepan, cover with water and bring to a boil. Reduce the heat and simmer for 30–45 minutes until soft. Drain and allow to cool slightly. When cool enough to handle, peel and core, then transfer to a blender or food processor and puree while still warm. Weigh the quince puree. **TWO** Place a quantity of granulated sugar equal in weight to the weight of the quince puree in a heavy saucepan, add the measured water, and heat slowly, stirring constantly, until the sugar has completely dissolved. **THREE** Increase the heat, bring to a boil and boil until the syrup reaches soft ball point (239°F, or when a drop will form a soft ball when dropped in cold water). Add the quince puree to the sugar syrup and cook, stirring constantly, for about 30 minutes until thick and the paste leaves the sides of the pan. **FOUR** Transfer the paste to a loaf pan lined with waxed paper and leave in a warm place for 3–4 days. Turn out onto a plate and allow to dry completely. You can then store the paste for up to 1 year in an airtight container. **FIVE** Slice and serve at room temperature with slices or shavings of Manchego cheese.

Makes 18 slices

NUTRIENT ANALYSIS PER SERVING 620 kJ – 146 cal – 0 g protein – 39 g carbohydrate – 39 g sugars – 0 g fat – 0 g saturated fat – 3 g fiber – 0 mg sodium

HEALTHY TIP Quinces are an excellent source of vitamin C, a powerful booster of the immune system and well known for their ability to increase resistance to infections and disease. They also contain fiber and riboflavin.

Roasted wild berries

A great variety of fruits grow in Mexico all year round and often seasonal fruits are the only item offered as dessert after a meal. In this recipe, the berries are lightly roasted to release their natural sweetness, resulting in an elegant and delicious dessert.

INGREDIENTS *1 cup small fresh strawberries ‖ ⅔ cup fresh blueberries ‖ 1 cup fresh raspberries ‖ ⅔ cup fresh blackberries ‖ 1 tablespoon superfine sugar (optional) ‖ mint sprigs, to decorate (optional)*

ONE Rinse and hull the strawberries and rinse the blueberries, then drain well and place on paper towels to dry. Gently wipe the raspberries and blackberries. **TWO** Gently warm the strawberries in a heavy saucepan over a medium heat, stirring constantly. Add the sugar, if using, then add the blueberries, raspberries, and blackberries and cook for about 1 minute; don't let the fruit become soggy. **THREE** Immediately transfer to a serving plate and decorate with mint sprigs, if liked. Serve warm.

Serves 4

NUTRIENT ANALYSIS PER SERVING 212 kJ – 50 cal – 1 g protein – 11 g carbohydrate – 11 g sugars – 0 g fat – 0 g saturated fat – 6 g fiber – 0 mg sodium

HEALTHY TIP This mix of berries is an excellent source of vitamins A and C, and rich in calcium, magnesium, potassium, beta-carotene, and folic acid.

Fresh fruit gelatin dessert

A particular favorite in Mexico, gelatin desserts are prepared for special occasions as well as everyday at lunchtime. Fruit gelatin desserts contain a generous amount of fresh fruit, the type of fruit used varying according to the season and family traditions.

INGREDIENTS *4 tablespoons water ‖ 5 teaspoons powdered gelatin ‖ 2 ½ cups cranberry juice ‖ ¼ cantaloupe melon, peeled and seeded (about 4 oz), diced ‖ ½ peeled and pitted mango (about 3 oz), diced ‖ 1 peeled and cored apple (about 3½ oz), diced ‖ 1 cup seedless red grapes ‖ 1 cup seedless green grapes ‖ ¾ cup fresh strawberries, hulled and quartered*

ONE Put the measured water in a small saucepan. Sprinkle over the gelatin and leave for 5 minutes until spongy. Place over a very low heat to dissolve, without either boiling or stirring, until it becomes liquid and clear. **TWO** Warm ⅔ cup of the cranberry juice and mix into the gelatin. Add the remaining cranberry juice and stir well. **THREE** Wet the base of individual bowls or an 8 inch diameter gelatin dessert mold and cover with some of the gelatin mixture. Chill in the refrigerator for about 20 minutes until beginning to set. **FOUR** Arrange the fruit over the gelatin, pour three quarters of the gelatin mixture over the fruit and refrigerate for about 20 minutes until beginning to set, then add the remaining mixture. (This is to ensure that the dessert has a flat base when turned out.) Refrigerate for 2–4 hours until completely set. **FIVE** Run the tip of a pointed knife around the edge of the mold to loosen. Place a damp serving plate over the mold and turn both the plate and mold over together. Give a sharp shake and lift the mold. Serve chilled.

Serves 6

NUTRIENT ANALYSIS PER SERVING 456 kJ – 107 cal – 2 g protein – 25 g carbohydrate – 14 g sugars – 0 g fat – 0 g saturated fat – 2 g fiber – 9 mg sodium

HEALTHY TIP While each type of fruit has its own specific composition of nutritional elements, fruit in general has certain common characteristics. Most fruits have a high water content and are a good source of vitamin A, vitamin B6, vitamin C, potassium, calcium, iron, and magnesium.

Corn cake

Corn cake is baked all over Mexico throughout the whole year, especially of course at harvest time, between July and September. It is usually served for breakfast or dinner with coffee or hot chocolate. It can be sweet or savory and sometimes it is offered as a side dish with mole sauce or poblano chili strips, as in central Mexico.

INGREDIENTS *3 cups fresh corn kernels* ‖ *¼ cup butter, melted, plus extra for greasing* ‖ *¼ cup superfine sugar* ‖ *½ cup all-purpose flour* ‖ *3 organic free-range eggs* ‖ *1 tablespoon baking powder* ‖ *¼ teaspoon salt* ‖ *1–2 tablespoons confectioners' sugar*

ONE Put the corn kernels in a blender or food processor and blend until smooth. Add all the remaining ingredients, except the confectioners' sugar, and process until well mixed. **TWO** Pour the mixture into a well-greased 8 inch diameter cake pan and bake in a preheated oven, 325°F, for about 35 minutes, or until a wooden toothpick inserted into the center comes out clean. **THREE** Remove from the oven and allow to rest for 10 minutes. Run the tip of a pointed knife around the edge of the pan to loosen the cake and invert onto a plate. Sift the confectioners' sugar on top. Serve warm.

Serves 6

NUTRIENT ANALYSIS PER SERVING 1236 kJ – 294 cal – 7 g protein – 38 g carbohydrate – 17 g sugars – 14 g fat – 7 g saturated fat – 3 g fiber – 454 mg sodium

HEALTHY TIP Corn contains beta-carotene, small amounts of B vitamins, and vitamins A and C. It is also a useful source of protein and rich in fiber.

Raspberry sorbet

Known in Mexico as *nieves*, sorbets are a traditional frozen dessert made with water, sugar, and fresh fruit. Raspberries are harvested during all the warmer months of the year; depending on the region, they are available from May through to November.

INGREDIENTS *3⅓ cups fresh raspberries* ‖ *¾ cup granulated sugar* ‖ *2 cups water* ‖ *freshly squeezed juice of ½ lime, or to taste* ‖ *mint sprigs, to decorate*

ONE Put the raspberries in a blender or food processor and blend to a puree. Pass through a strainer and set aside. **TWO** Put the sugar in a heavy saucepan, add the measured water and heat over a low heat, stirring constantly, until the sugar has completely dissolved. Increase the heat, bring to a boil, and gently boil for 5 minutes. Remove from the heat and add the raspberry puree and lime juice. **THREE** Freeze the raspberry mixture in an ice-cream maker according to the manufacturer's instructions. Alternatively, pour into a shallow, freezerproof container and freeze for about 1 hour until beginning to solidify. Return to the blender or the food processor and blend to break up the ice crystals. Return to the container and freeze again for 3–4 hours until firm. **FOUR** Serve in scoops, decorated with mint sprigs.

Serves 4

NUTRIENT ANALYSIS PER SERVING 740 kJ – 173 cal – 1 g protein – 44 g carbohydrate – 44 g sugars – 0 g fat – 0 g saturated fat – 7 g fiber – 0 mg sodium

HEALTHY TIP Raspberries are an excellent source of calcium, magnesium, phosphorus, potassium, and vitamins B3 and C. They also are an effective antioxidant and astringent.

Mango sorbet

Fruit sorbets are very popular throughout the country and different regions have developed their own varieties according to the season and the local fruits. In the state of Veracruz, mango sorbet is one of the most popular flavors sold by street vendors.

INGREDIENTS *5–6 ripe mangoes ‖ 3 tablespoons granulated sugar, or to taste ‖ 3 tablespoons water ‖ a few drops of freshly squeezed lime juice, or to taste ‖ mint sprigs, to decorate (optional)*

ONE Peel the mangoes, remove the flesh and put in a blender or food processor with the sugar, measured water, and lime juice. Blend until smooth. Taste and add more sugar or lime juice as necessary. **TWO** Freeze the mango mixture in an ice-cream maker according to the manufacturer's instructions. Alternatively, pour into a shallow, freezerproof container and freeze for about 1 hour until beginning to solidify. Return to the blender or food processor and blend to break up the ice crystals. Return to the container and freeze again for 3–4 hours until firm. **THREE** Serve in scoops, decorated with mint sprigs, if desired.

Serves 4

NUTRIENT ANALYSIS PER SERVING 710 kJ – 166 cal – 1 g protein – 42 g carbohydrate – 42 g sugars – 0 g fat – 0 g saturated fat – 5 g fiber – 4 mg sodium

HEALTHY TIP In addition to their exquisite and delicate taste, mangoes are an excellent source of vitamins A and C.

Margarita tequila cocktail

The famed Mexican cocktail Margarita is very popular in bars and restaurants all over the country. Combining tequila, lime juice, sugar syrup, and orange-flavored liqueur, it is traditionally served in a glass that has had its rim dipped in lime juice and then coated with salt.

INGREDIENTS *12 oz ice cubes* ‖ *½ cup white tequila* ‖ *½ cup Cointreau* ‖ *½ cup freshly squeezed lime juice* ‖ *¼ cup sugar syrup*

TO SERVE *lime wedges, for preparing the glasses and to decorate* ‖ *salt, for preparing the glasses*

ONE Rub the rims of 4 Martini glasses with a lime wedge, then dip lightly into a dish of salt. **TWO** Place the ice cubes in a blender, add the tequila, Cointreau, lime juice, and sugar syrup and blend at high speed for 30 seconds. **THREE** Pour the tequila mixture into the prepared glasses, decorate with lime wedges and serve immediately.

Serves 4

NUTRIENT ANALYSIS PER SERVING 825 kJ – 200 cal – 0 g protein – 16 g carbohydrate – 16 g sugars – 0 g fat – 0 g saturated fat – 0 g fiber – 0 mg sodium

HEALTHY TIP As with all alcoholic beverages, this cocktail must be consumed in moderation. However, the vitamin C from the lime can be helpful in protecting the body from some of the harmful effects of the alcohol. If you are concerned about your salt intake, omit the salt on the glass rim.

Christmas hot punch

This is the most popular drink served in Mexico during the Christmas and New Year festivities, prepared with seasonal fruits cooked in water with cinnamon and raw sugar. Adults drink the punch with *piquete*, which means that it is laced with alcohol. Sugar cane stalks are available from West Indian food stores.

INGREDIENTS *10 cups water* ‖ *8 pitted prunes* ‖ *10 organic dried apricots, quartered* ‖ *3 guavas, quartered* ‖ *4 oz sugar cane stalks, peeled and cut into strips* ‖ *2 oz dried hibiscus flowers* ‖ *1 apple, cored and cut into 8 segments* ‖ *1 tablespoon raisins* ‖ *1–2 cinnamon sticks* ‖ *⅓ cup superfine sugar, or to taste* ‖ *½ cup dark rum, or to taste*

ONE Bring the measured water to a boil in a large saucepan over a high heat. Add the prunes and apricots, reduce the heat and simmer for 5 minutes. Add the guavas, sugar cane, hibiscus, apple, raisins, cinnamon sticks, and sugar and simmer over a low heat for 30 minutes, stirring occasionally. Taste the punch and add a little more sugar if necessary. Stir well. **TWO** Remove from the heat, add the rum, and stir well. **THREE** Ladle into individual mugs and serve immediately.

Serves 6–8

NUTRIENT ANALYSIS PER SERVING 690 kJ – 163 cal – 1 g protein – 30 g carbohydrate – 30 g sugars – 0 g fat – 0 g saturated fat – 6 g fiber – 13 mg sodium

HEALTHY TIP This punch contains several healthy fruits. The guava is an outstanding source of vitamin C and soluble fiber, while the raisins, prunes, and apricots all have valuable antioxidant effects in the inhibiting and controlling of the harmful action of free radicals.

Sangrita tequila chaser

Whenever you ask for tequila in bars and restaurants in Mexico, it will usually be served accompanied with a *sangrita* (little blood). Each restaurant has its own recipe, but this sweet and spicy, red beverage is typically a blended mixture of tomato, orange, and lime juice and is seasoned with salt and chili.

INGREDIENTS *1 cup tomato juice* ‖ *¼ cup freshly squeezed orange juice* ‖ *2 tablespoons freshly squeezed lime juice* ‖ *1 tablespoon finely chopped onion* ‖ *1 teaspoon finely chopped green chili (seeded for a milder taste)* ‖ *salt and freshly ground black pepper* ‖ *tequila, to serve*

ONE Place all the ingredients in a blender and blend to puree. Check the seasoning. Cover and chill in the refrigerator until required. **TWO** Serve chilled with a shot of your favorite tequila.

Serves 4

NUTRIENT ANALYSIS PER SERVING 69 kJ – 16 cal – 1 g protein – 4 g carbohydrate – 3 g sugars – 0 g fat – 0 g saturated fat – 0 g fiber – 144 mg sodium

HEALTHY TIP The healthy tomato juice is enriched with the nutrients from the orange and lime juice, making this drink a potent antiseptic beverage.

Hot chocolate

Cacao is one of the most important Mexican contributions to the gastronomic world. Chocolate is a pre-Hispanic ritual beverage, made with cacao and water, served cold with plenty of foam. The present practice of using milk and serving it hot is widely accepted. One of the most popular chocolate bars used to prepare this drink contains ground cacao, sugar, cinnamon, almond, and vanilla.

INGREDIENTS *4 cups lowfat milk or water* ‖ *6 oz bittersweet chocolate, containing at least 55% cocoa solids, chopped*

ONE Heat the milk or water with the chocolate in a saucepan over a medium heat. Bring to a boil and remove the pan from the heat. **TWO** Using a whisk, beat the chocolate mixture vigorously until the chocolate has completely melted and a thick layer of foam has formed over the surface. **THREE** Pour the chocolate into individual cups and serve immediately.

Serves 4

NUTRIENT ANALYSIS PER SERVING 1310 kJ – 312 cal – 10 g protein – 37 g carbohydrate – 35 g sugars – 15 g fat – 9 g saturated fat – 0 g fiber – 140 mg sodium

HEALTHY TIP In spite of their fat content, cocoa beans are rather nutritious; they supply useful amounts of proteins, some B vitamins, and trace elements, particularly iron and magnesium. Chocolate can give a short-lived boost of energy because of its sugar content. It should be drunk in moderation.

Acknowledgments

EXECUTIVE EDITOR Nicky Hill

PROJECT EDITORS Leanne Bryan and Ruth Hamilton

DEPUTY CREATIVE DIRECTOR Karen Sawyer

DESIGNER Janis Utton

SENIOR PRODUCTION CONTROLLER Manjit Sihra

PHOTOGRAPHY Emma Neish / © Octopus Publishing Group Ltd

FOOD STYLIST Sunil Vijayakar

PROPS STYLIST Liz Hippisley

Picture acknowledgments

Special Photography: © **Octopus Publishing Group Limited**/Emma Neish